A Primer On Pain

DISCOVER HOW SUFFERING SHAPES OUR LIVES

To Joseph
Keep Believing!

Scott Camp

Scott Camp
PS 25:18

Franklin Publishing

PRINCETON, TEXAS

Kelly Carr / Franklin Publishing
1215 Juniper
Princeton, Texas 75407

www.FranklinPublishing.org

Ordering Information:

Quantity sales. Special discounts are available on quantity purchases by corporations, associations, and others. For details, contact Scott Camp by email at camp.scott.r@gmail.com.

Except where otherwise indicated, all Scripture quotations are taken from the New King James Version®. Copyright © 1982 by Thomas Nelson. Used by permission. All rights reserved.

A Primer On Pain: Discover How Suffering Shapes Our Lives / Scott Camp. —1st ed.

Testimonials

Scott Camp's wonderful book on pain couldn't be more relevant considering the times in which we live. He speaks with integrity from his own hardship, inviting readers to walk alongside him in his effort to glean wisdom from the Scriptures concerning the causes and function of pain in the world. By reading this reflection, readers are sure to come away with a storehouse of wisdom about God and obedience to the divine will where we need it most.

—Frank D. Macchia, D. Theol., D.D.
Professor of Systematic Theology,
Vanguard University

Scott Camp's book on pain is one of the most moving works on the subject I have ever read. It is theologically substantive yet carefully interwoven with profound personal anecdotes and compelling life stories that make what are usually difficult spiritual issues to take on an unparalleled poignancy. It is perhaps C.S. Lewis updated to our own troubling times.

—Carl Raschke, Ph.D.
Professor of Philosophy,
University of Denver
Author, The Next Reformation

I have often found not only God's purpose but also His power in times of pain. Scott Camp has insight that gives a different perspective on life's challenges that can serve as great encouragement.

—Dr. Johnny Hunt
Evangelism Director,
North American Mission Board
Pastor Emeritus,
FBC Woodstock, GA
Past President, SBC

There are few greater mysteries in life than the problem of pain. It comes in many forms and has many causes, but in every case the challenge to us is the same—how do we deal with it? In this book, Scott Camp covers the ground, gives relevant examples, and points us to the ways in which we can confront the issues and resolve them. This is a book to read, to give to those who are suffering, and to keep for the times when it will be needed in our own lives.

—Gerald Bray, D.Litt.
Research Professor of Divinity,
Beeson Divinity School/Samford University
Birmingham, AL

In a world groaning for redemption (Rom. 8:18-21), every human being experiences pain, and—more often than we care to admit—we often cause others pain. In *A Primer on Pain*, Camp weaves together his own stories with biblical instruction and the experiences of others, drawing the reader into a theology of suffering through vulnerability and openness. His goal is not to induce sympathy or pity but to direct others toward a path of healing and redemption. He avoids trite clichés and emotional manipulation as he encourages readers to trust in a good God who has promised to make all things new. Pain is not purposeless or meaningless; suffering is not caused by God, but God has a purpose in allowing pain and suffering to exist and persist. The hope of resurrection and recreation of all things gives us hope in the journey. Like our Savior, we can endure suffering for the joy set before us (Heb. 12:1-3).

—Glenn R. Kreider, Ph.D.
Professor of Theological Studies,
Dallas Theological Seminary

A Primer on Pain is a personal and timely word from Scott Camp for those challenging times in life characterized by struggle, suffering, disappointment, and pain. Reflective, confessional, and informed by Scripture, Camp seeks to offer encouragement and guidance for the difficult seasons and dark days that come our way. Concluding with a thoughtful exposition of James 1, our author points readers in the direction of joy, character development, perseverance, wisdom, and song, offering help and hope that is found in the providential grace and mercy of the self-revealing Triune God.

—David S. Dockery, Ph.D.
Distinguished Professor of Theology,
Southwestern Baptist Theological Seminary
President, International Alliance for Christian Education

A Primer on Pain seeks neither to emulate the rarified philosophical heights of the argumentation of C.S. Lewis's *The Problem of Pain* or plumb the raw emotional depths of Lewis's later *A Grief Observed*. As admired as Lewis is by many Christians, though, the vast majority of believers are not looking for apologetic intellectual brilliance or to be further unsettled emotionally when they are in the midst of their own acute pain. Neither are they looking for opportunities to counsel someone else who is suffering and/or struggling in their faith as a result of such suffering. Scott Camp's *Primer* is wisely insightful and unvarnished "real life" that speaks loud and clear to those who desperately need such help. This slender volume is the eloquent testimony of one who has been through the refining fire of suffering and learned well its hard, but precious, lessons.

—Boyd Luter, Ph.D.
Professor of Biblical Studies, The King's University

I was deeply moved yet also greatly encouraged while reading *A Primer on Pain*. Anyone experiencing pain in life has wrestled with the question of why. Ironically, that question can be more challenging to those who believe in a loving God. Books written from a purely philosophical perspective or a theological perspective devoid of real-life application are sometimes inadequate to help the one wrestling with painful issues. Scott Camp's openness to share heart-wrenching events in his personal life demonstrates that he is well acquainted with the tough questions arising from painful circumstances. Scott's greatest contribution to the reader is his articulation of sound and practical scriptural truths that have not only been the source of understanding and comfort in his own life but that can be a source of help to all of us who have or will wrestle with pain.

—Kermit Bridges, D.Min.
President, Southwestern Assemblies of God University,
Waxahachie, TX

One of the glaring deficiencies of the Western Church has been the lack of a cohesive theology of suffering. In fact, some have even inferred that Christians who suffer are somehow lacking in spirituality. Scott Camp addresses the conundrum of suffering, which is the most shared of all human experiences, in this exceptionally sensitive, insightful book. Drawing from his own crucible of loss with deep vulnerability, pastoral concern, and thorough theological undergirding, Dr. Camp has given us a treasure. The contents of *A Primer on Pain* are so rich and so helpful that it is surely destined to become a classic.

—David Shibley

Founder and World Representative,
Global Advance

Scott Camp has written a biblically based confessional theology on the subject of pain. It is in his words "a non-philosophical yet biblically rooted theodicy." Every believer struggles to understand the presence of pain and suffering while also believing in a God who is all-powerful and full of grace. In the six chapters of *A Primer on Pain*, Scott interweaves painful experiences from his own life along with biblical examples including Job, David, Paul, and the City of Smyrna that endured persecution. The human, even the Christian, life is not without pain and suffering. The author relates reasons behind our pain, which include the fall of humanity, the influence of Satan, self-inflicted pain, and persecution in many places in the world. Woven into his *Primer on Pain*, Camp has given hope through brokenness, repentance, and restoration. The book ends with a strong affirmation that God is going to bring us through our painful experiences, "better, not bitter; victorious, not victims!" This book is a timely word for this season!

—Dr. Gaylan D. Claunch
Assemblies of God Superintendent,
North Texas District
Waxahachie, TX

I knew before I finished the first chapter of *A Primer on Pain* that I would be buying multiple copies of this book to give away to people who are experiencing pain. I have been a pastor for over forty years. Scott's book deals with questions every pastor must answer when shepherding people through life. I loved the way Scott combined his scholarly insight with his personal experiences of pain. He deals with pain from all angles and offers practical biblical solutions to each scenario. Here is a book for everyone because it offers clear insights into the problem of pain and suffering.

—Rev. Pepper Puryear
Senior Pastor,
First Baptist Church
Mt Vernon, TX

This powerful description of pain will change your life and give you a simple yet profound understanding of pain. It will shift your spirit and your way of thinking about trials and setbacks. After reading *A Primer on Pain*, you will be invigorated to stop running away from fear and pain and use it as a catalyst to propel you to your next dimension. Dr. Camp explains the different forms of pain that come to us all, in various manners and shapes, even to the strongest among us. Dr. Camp writes with simplicity, but the book's words will empower you to understand that a relationship with Christ does not bring immunity from pain but allow you to handle it with victory assured, at some period in that experience. This book explains how 'these trials of life' can foist themselves on us, yet if responded to authentically and with strength from above, can make us stronger at the end. It is a beautifully written book from Dr. Camp's heart, and its contents speak volumes of his own valley/pain experience. His use of biblical in-sights and personal experience bring a fresh look at this subject. This book will change your life. I highly recommend you get it immediately before 2020 is over or early 2021!

—Pastor Joe Persaud
Lead Pastor, Liberty Church NY
Founder, Hope is Rising Global

Scott Camp has clean hands and a pure heart. He has been forged in the fires of life and presents a wonderful book on the theology of suffering. I recommend you read *A Primer on Pain* and pray, "Lord, let your will and not my will be done."

—Bishop Walter Harvey
President,
National Black Fellowship of the Assemblies of God
Milwaukee, WI

Scott Camp's *A Primer on Pain* is much needed in these difficult times. It provides understanding, strength, and comfort for the sufferer and wisdom and guidance for the caregiver.

—Pastor Richard Exley
Author of When You Lose Someone You Love

I read this book through tears, stopping several times to regain my ability to focus. Scott took me to places I have known and experienced as a man and a pastor. His potent combination of writing that embraces his pastoral and evangelistic experience plus his academic background brings the reader into this intense subject. His willingness to be transparent and vulnerable empowers the possibility of healing in others. I am better for reading *A Primer on Pain* and plan to lead the people of Seaport through its pages.

—Brad Whipple
Pastor, Seaport Community Church
Presbyter, AG of New England
Groton, CT

Our society's natural default position about pain is to avoid it at all costs. Most books on pain are strategies to avoid or eliminate it from our lives. Scott Camp describes his new book as both confessional and a theology. In short, he recognizes pain is part of human experience. He also affirms that God's perspective on that experience is important. The result is a book that looks pain straight in the eye and offers the possibility of living through pain. There is a God who assures us that our lives are not in vain, doomed, or worthless. Turns out this book is more than a primer; it is a theological textbook.

—Byron D. Klaus, D.Min.
President,
Assemblies of God Theological Seminary (1999-2015)
Springfield, MO

Shocking. Simple. Surprised. Dr. Scott Camp reveals a truth that pain happens to us all through his own amazing journey of pain—and healing. His revelation of God's eternal truths about pain and healing seem so simple yet reveal a surprising depth of understanding in the all-powerful healing balm of God's grace through Scott's own traumatic experiences. A captivating story of changed lives and biblical truths that will transform your heart and leave you changed—for eternity.

—Marshall M. Windsor, D.Min.
Evangelist, Author, Educator
Past National Evangelist Representative
Assemblies of God

Dr. Scott Camp's theological reflection on the sources of pain omits the cold and distant philosophical approach I have come to associate with books on pain. Instead, this book stays close to the ground, where pain and suffering touch us all. The honesty and humility with which Dr. Camp recounts his own experiences of pain invite readers to courageously face their own most painful experiences, held by the supporting power that the Holy Spirit provides even in the depths of horror and grief.

—Alan Jay Richard, Ph.D.
Author, Educator, Christian Activist

When our pain intensifies, we often medicate rather than meditate because it's easier to cover the symptoms than to confront the sources. In *A Primer on Pain*, Scott Camp—with a riveting yet easy-to-understand writing style—gives us six sources for our suffering. As you contemplate the truth in this primer, hope will begin to emerge. Jesus heals, but the mist in our eyes means we might miss Him. *A Primer on Pain* ensures you don't, and I predict it will be used by God to bring healing to the souls of many.

—**Wade Burleson**
Sr. Pastor,
Emmanuel Baptist Church, Enid, OK
Past President,
Baptist General Convention of Oklahoma

When Scott, my longtime friend and former Associate, asked me to review his latest book, *A Primer on Pain*, I thought I would just glance at the first chapter and then read it when I had the time, but it captured my attention to the point that I had to keep reading to the end. I believe you will have the same experience. If you have ever had suffering and pain in your life, you *must* read this book. As long as the wounds of the past are still open, you will continue to have suffering, pain, and bitterness. In this book, you will learn to turn your wounds into scars and live with them victoriously.

—**Dr. Charles Massegee**
Evangelist and Author
President, CMEA
Past President, SBC Conference of Evangelists

I've just finished reading *A Primer in Pain* by Dr. Scott Camp. Once I read the first few pages, I could not stop reading. The writer's insight into the incredible subject of suffering, trials, brokenness, and faith is both convicting and inspiring. At times, I felt like weeping, and at times I felt like shouting for joy. The author's honesty and transparency are refreshing. Every young preacher should read this book, and it will bless greatly many of us who are not so young.

—**Dr. Don Paul Gray**
President,
JSBC
Baton Rouge, LA

In a rare approach to the subject of pain, Scott Camp delivers part memoir, part biblical exposition, walking with us as we recover from personal pain. He takes us through some of his own painful situations, in which you may see glimpses of yourself. It is well researched both biblically and through other Christian voices from past to present. You may cry, but you will heal more as a result of reading this book. I did.

—**Bruce Coats, Ph.D.**
Dean, Winebrenner Theological Seminary
Findlay, OH

Biblical, practical, pastoral, vulnerable, helpful—this primer on pain is written by a man who has walked through the valley of the shadow of death and come out the other side finding God to be faithful through it all. Pain in life is not a matter of *if* but *when*. When you walk through pain, have this book handy. It will minister to your soul.

—Dr. Andrew Hébert
Lead Pastor, Paramount Baptist Church, Amarillo, Texas

With a pastor's heart, Scott Camp leads readers through a discovery of the sources of our pain and God's redemptive solution. *A Primer on Pain* is theological, practical, and beautiful, weaving together firsthand accounts with the greater story of God's grace and purpose in our lives. This book will move you to think better about what God is doing during the worst of times to bring about His best.

Dr. David Daniels
Lead Pastor, Central Bible Church, Arlington, TX

Divorce, abuse, death, and failure afflict the human family. All these have afflicted Scott Camp as well. In *A Primer on Pain*, Scott blends careful hand-ling of the biblical text with personal, painful illustrations from his own story to provide a path to victory for readers. While Scott and I view the Spirit's gifts differently, I can heartily commend his work to anyone who has suffered. Through all your wailing, lamenting, and hurting, Scott's book will shepherd readers to a place of peace and strength.

—David Mills, Ph.D.
Sr. Pastor,
Beech Haven Baptist Church, Athens, GA
Former Professor of Evangelism, SWBTS

A Primer on Pain tells the story of God's grace in the middle of suffering through the crucible of my friend and brother Scott Camp's life. I am grateful for this, as it has brought comfort and clarity in my own return to the Lord. Scott not only writes about suffering in its various forms; he also lives out the wisdom he shares. When I was at the bottom, lamenting my sin and failure, and hanging onto grace for dear life, Scott found me and continues to walk with me. Read this book. Find God's grace afresh. But also learn from it how to love those who continue to walk in brokenness, and those who suffer alone.

—Alvin Reid, Ph.D.
Writer, Editor, Researcher
Former Chair, Bailey Smith School of Evangelism
Southeastern Baptist Theological Seminary

A Primer on Pain by my friend, Scott Camp, is destined to bring clear insight, hope, and healing to thousands of hurting people. Instead of preaching from a high pulpit, Scott writes with transparency from his own painful experiences. He answers hard questions with biblically sound theology. His passion for seeing people drawn to Christ for ultimate healing flows from his heart as an evangelist. Please share this powerful book with every hurting person you know.

Dr. Wayne Bristow
International Evangelist
Director of Evangelism,
Baptist General Convention of Oklahoma (retired)

In *A Primer on Pain*, Scott Camp broaches an unexplored topic within many Christian circles: pain and suffering. He sensitively shares painful moments in his life and the lives of others. He weaves these stories of suffering insightfully within biblical, historical, and theological frameworks. While there will be readers who will question interpretations offered by Camp, this book will offer readers a vital set of questions, analyses, and insight about pain and suffering from an informed and thoughtful Christian perspective.

Dr. David D. Daniels III
Henry Luce Professor of Church History
McCormick Seminary, Chicago, IL
Bishop COGIC

Dedication

The book is dedicated to

Ernest Carter

Michelle Chaney

Michael Freeman

Lindsay Kimmons

Amanda Maxwell

Casualties of War

Until then...

Contents

Foreword

The world is a dangerous place, and we must learn to navigate our way around its pitfalls. Even then, however, some pain and suffering cannot be avoided.

As I write this Foreword to Scott Camp's insightful book, *A Primer On Pain: Discover How Suffering Shapes Our Lives*, an aggressive novel virus is sweeping across the globe, infecting great swaths of society, and leaving sickness and death in its wake. COVID-19 is no respecter of persons and knows no borders—religious, racial, ethnic, geographic, or political.

In the midst of a widespread pandemic, most people turn to their governmental leaders for answers and assistance. Yet their help is limited at best. Scientists are working overtime to discover a cure or produce a vaccine. By the time you read these words, COVID may still be killing multitudes.

Christians are not immune to pain. Like everyone else, we suffer "the slings and arrows" that are pointed in our direction.

A Primer On Pain is an important book, which I believe will stand the test of time. Drawing on both scholarly and popular sources, Scott Camp tackles the problem of human suffering. He does not, however, offer simplistic or glib answers to the most profound of questions: "Why do the righteous suffer?" Rather, he offers hope to those in pain and provides ways to cope when it knocks at our door.

A former professor of mine once said, "All good theology is practical theology." Unless our theology speaks to real life situations, it remains speculative and theoretical. *A Primer On Pain* contains good theology. Within its pages, the rubber meets the road.

Camp introduces us to many kinds of pain. For instance, "When Others Cause You Pain" (chapter 1) focuses on the issue of victimization and turns to the story of Joseph, who after being sold into slavery and placed in prison emerged stronger as a consequence. Joseph discovered the secret of forgiveness. In like manner, Jesus was a victim of violence who prayed, "Father forgive them" (Luke 23:34).

Scott Camp devotes two chapters to Satan, the epitome of evil whose goal is "to kill, steal, and destroy" (John 10:10). When faced with pure evil how should we respond? To teach us the lesson, Job steps onto center stage. When stripped of his comforts, possessions, and physical strength, Job faced the indignity of well-meaning friends who delivered up more pain than comfort. Only when Job argued with God do we learn that Satan was behind Job's troubles. God set the record straight and promised to intervene.

Camp reminds us that some suffering is self-inflicted and a result of our own sinful choices. Who better than King David to teach us about repentance and restoration? Even after finding our way back to God, however, we may still be left with terrible consequences as David was.

Pain is not only a reality; it is woven into the fabric of this "present age" and touches us all. There is no escape. Adam's sin and the resultant Fall have thrown creation into a tailspin, leaving earth's inhabitants in a state of constant groaning. Camp shows us that while we traverse this planet, only God's grace can sustain us.

Persecution is a special category of pain reserved for those saints living under oppressive regimes. From the days of Peter and Paul up to the present, some believers have been crucified, burned, tortured, and beheaded for their faith. Looking to the Apocalypse, a book written by the hand of the Apostle John—a man exiled for Christ, Scott Camp finds ultimate hope in the arrival of a new heaven and new earth, when God creates for His children new bodies that cannot be destroyed.

When facing political execution for His unwavering faithfulness, Jesus cried from the Cross, "My God, my God, why have you forsaken me?" (Matt 27:46). Instead of responding with a theological answer, God in His time intervened on Christ's behalf and raised him from the dead.

How should the resurrection of Jesus change our own perspective on pain and suffering? If we expect an answer to the "Why" question, we will be sorely disappointed. If we expect that our earthly pain will suddenly disappear, we will become disillusioned. But if we turn to the God who raised Christ from the dead, we can face life's pain, knowing that one day we too will be raised.

Reader, you are in for a treat. *A Primer On Pain* is filled with encouragement, real-life stories, pithy statements, biblical illustrations, and practical advice on how to face pain. Within these pages you will be moved to tears and then to laughter. But most of all, you will feel God's love and comfort.

If you are sick or sad, if you have been wronged or betrayed, if you have suffered for your commitment to Jesus, or if you simply struggle one day at a time to survive, this book is for you.

A Primer On Pain will be the best and most practical book you will read this year.

—R. Alan Streett, PhD
Senior Research Professor of Biblical Theology,
Criswell College, Dallas, Texas

PREFACE

I am writing this primer in the midst of the COVID-19 pandemic, perhaps the most lethal virus in 100 years. All of us (and I am speaking as a citizen of the world) have been impacted and have felt the pain of over one million deaths worldwide at the time of this writing.

What is pain *for*? Is there some grand overarching meaningful purpose for the things we suffer in this life? Or are we, in the words of C. S. Lewis, "rats in a trap"? Or worse, "rats in a laboratory"?[1]

I am writing as a Christian—in fact, as an ordained minister for almost forty years. A large part of being a minister is dealing with pain and suffering. Endless rounds of hospital visits, funerals, suicides, cancer, abuse of every imaginable variety, divorce, domestic violence, collapse of business, the shattering of hopes and dreams ... need I go on? *To be human is to suffer.* Christianity is no escape from the vicissitudes and tragedies of life. Anyone who tells you different is not an honest broker.

I have had my own share of pain and the brokenness that results. I am writing this book, in part, as a kind of catharsis. My earliest memories are filled with pain. My relationship with Christ, my marriage to wonderful Gina, my immediate family, and the Christian community have all contributed to my healing over the years. I'm already, but not yet, whole. I am, like you, a wounded healer. In that sense, we are like

Christ. He was "a man of sorrows, acquainted with grief" (Isa. 53:3).

My prayer is that this "little book" (primer) will be an aid on your journey toward healing from hurts that are an inevitable part of life as we know it: life on a broken planet, inhabited by broken, fallen, and hurting people who often inflict their pain on us. It is often said that "hurt people hurt people." This is true. It seems we have one of two choices in life. We can, by faith, allow the Spirit to begin the healing process and "help us in our infirmities" to become better, or we can isolate ourselves, hiding even from God and become brittle and bitter (Rom. 8:26).

My prayer is that the writing (my part) and reading (your part) of this book will help us become better. It is to this end that I offer up this, my contribution, to the "endless making of books" (Eccl. 12:12).

Scott Camp

September 11, 2020

ACKNOWLEDGMENTS

Nothing worth doing can be done without the help of others. I would like to acknowledge the help of two of my sons.

Joshua Camp is a brilliant young man whose love of the biblical text, clarity of thought, and use of the English language far surpasses my own. I am especially proud to be known as his father. His reworking of large parts of the original manuscript which I wrote by hand on a yellow legal pad has been a labor of love for "dear ole Dad." I look forward to years of literary output in a variety of genres, including musical, from Josh. I love you, son!

I would also like to acknowledge a "son in the ministry" whom I have come to love dearly in the Gospel, David Bumgardner. David is an excellent thinker and burgeoning systematic and biblical theologian whose aid has been immeasurable throughout this project. Thank you, David!

These two "Gen Zers" give me a renewed hope that a new "Jesus Movement" is on the horizon for my country. They will certainly be at the forefront. Besides being academics, they both share my passion for evangelism and spiritual awakening in the United States.

INTRODUCTION

I am writing *A Primer On Pain* as a confessional theology of suffering. I am also writing this book as a non-philosophical, biblical theodicy. Let me briefly explain what I mean by these terms.

This book is *confessional* in its approach. It is a book about my own painful journey of faith. I want to encourage you, the reader (whatever your context), by being brutally honest regarding my own pain. I am doing so in the hope that you will continue your pilgrim-age with full assurance that you, by the grace of our Lord, can make it through your present circumstances. God can use your pain to make you more like Jesus. This, after all, is the goal of God and the desire of every child of God: to be like Jesus. He has used my pain so repeatedly in my life for this very purpose. Someone has rightly noted, "God hits straight licks with crooked sticks." Not every painful experience comes directly from God. As a matter of fact, I propose in this *Primer* that most experiences do not come directly from Him, and yet, He still can use bad things for our good. So, in this little book, I'll share my own story and make my confession that *Jesus is Lord*—even in the painful seasons of our lives.

This book is a *theology of suffering*. In developing this theology, I seek to understand the sources of the pain we suffer.

Chapter 1 deals with the pain and suffering we experience at the hands of others. Here I relate the story of a dysfunctional and painful childhood.

Beginning in chapter 2 and continuing into chapter 3, I delve into the sinister nature of Satan's attack on all of God's good creation, including Satan's very personal attacks on believers. Here I share the devastating story of the Metro Church bus crash.

Chapter 4 is the most personal and pain-filled chapter for me. I conclude that most of the pain we suffer is the result of our own sinful choices. I am no exception.

Chapter 5 deals with what I have termed the *now-season* of suffering, which is common to all men since the Fall and from which there is no escape this side of the consummation of the kingdom of God. This consummation, which constitutes our hope, I term the *New Season.*

Chapter 6 looks at persecution. The pain that results in being persecuted for the cause of Christ is currently being experienced in unprecedented ways around the world. It may soon be the lot of those of us who have been, for the most part, sheltered from this in the West. This chapter contains a serious exegesis of a section of text in The Apocalypse. Therefore, it might take a bit more effort to read. I trust it is worthy of your time.

These are the *sources* of pain as I see it. I am not dealing with physical pain, *per se.*[2]

This book is also a non-philosophical yet biblically rooted theodicy. How can God be *both* all-powerful and all benevolent in the face of such pain? This is the question with which philosophers have wrestled for centuries. I am certainly aware of the literature written on this topic by academicians.[3] This is typically, at least in the Christian context, the work of professional apologists. I have great respect and admiration for their work. I consider much of their contribution a gift of God to the world. I have taught apologetics at the college level for several years, but this approach is not my purpose. I am engaging more with the text of Scripture and, in most instances, with the biblical narratives that give us wisdom and from which we glean principles to help us deal with our pain in productive ways.[4]

I believe that God is *justified*—that He is righteous in both allowing suffering and using suffering and the pain which results for His glory as well as our good.

I am, of course, first and foremost a preacher, and an evangelist to boot. So, at times, you may "hear" this coming through the page and feel as if you're at a revival meeting or evangelistic crusade. This is particularly true of the Conclusion, which is based on a message I preached recently at Calvary Chapel in Houston, Texas. When I extended the invitation to receive Christ, hundreds responded. I pray that God will speak to you in the course of reading this book. When He does, respond accordingly: set the book aside and do business with God!

1

When Others Cause You Pain

*"Life IS pain, highness. Anyone who says different is
selling something."*

—Westley to the Princess in *The Princess Bride*

Gina and I love going to the movies. The experience provides
a kind of therapy for me and a break from the intensity of
ministry. This was especially true in the early days of our marriage. We both like light-hearted comedies and thought that
was what we were in for one afternoon in the mid-nineties.
"Bye Bye Love" was billed as a romantic comedy and starred
some of our favorite television actors who were, many for the
first time, coming to the big screen. I had no idea what the
central theme of the film was, nor did I anticipate the impact
this low-budget, little-known movie would have on my life
that day. The movie is about divorce, particularly about its impact on children. Even as I write, I find myself stirred to tears
recalling the faded memory of my parents' final days as ...

well, my parents—at least as I had known them to be up until that time.

My mother was a beautiful woman. She was also deeply broken. Years into my adulthood she would recount to me the story of her own dysfunctional childhood and sexual abuse. She met my dad (himself a teenager) and was pregnant and married by age sixteen. Thus, began our happy little family— fatally flawed from the start. Two half-sisters would be born from adulterous relationships over the next six years. And then it all ended.

Back to the movie. As I watched, I was reliving every painful moment; waves of uncontrolled emotion came crashing over rocks submerged in the psyche of my pain-filled soul. I began to weep openly. I was inconsolable. My poor wife! We had entered the theatre with popcorn and soft drink in hand in order to escape reality. Now things were more real than ever before. I sat, all six feet and 230 pounds of me, crying like a little boy being pounded by bullies on a schoolyard playground. Gina lovingly and patiently tried her best to comfort my broken heart with whispers of, "Honey, it's okay. I'm here. This movie brought up some awful memories, didn't it? Would you like to leave?"

Painful childhood memories sometimes erupt like this: unanticipated, unwanted, and unwelcomed. In fact, some of our most severe hurts are inflicted upon us by those closest to us. This is why the home is so important; the family serves as the foundation needed by a child to grow into a responsible and productive adult. Children need the "roots" of stability that come from the experience of seeing parents who love unconditionally. They also need "wings," that is, a vision of what their lives can become.

God designed that this healthy sense of self should come through our parents. This kind of confidence is channeled through years of receiving the right kind of affirmation. The Bible speaks of the importance and significance of receiving this blessing from our mother and father. Gary Smalley helps us understand this need. Drawing from the Old Testament concept of the parental blessing, Smalley defines its key elements as beginning

> with meaningful touching [by which he means kissing, hugging, or the laying on of hands]. It continues with a spoken message of high value, a message that pictures a special future for the individual being blessed, and one that is based on an active commitment to see the blessing come to pass. ... We all have a powerful need to know that someone loves us and accepts us unconditionally. We especially crave our parents' blessing, and without it, we may become angry and driven or detached and empty.[5]

I did not receive such nurture. My roots were ripped up, my wings were clipped, and my blessing was withheld. My parents were too young and too inexperienced in the ways of life to understand the damage their actions would have on my sisters and me. I get that now. I am a husband, father, grandfather, professor, and minister. Back then I was a hurting little boy, vulnerable and looking for acceptance from anyone who offered it. Unfortunately, this acceptance came in the form of an older family member who would exploit my vulnerability for his own twisted, predatory pleasure. Of course, I am speaking here of sexual abuse.

I was no stranger to sexuality. At a young age I was exposed to the seemingly endless affairs of my mother. I would be left unsupervised often for days at a time in the midst of parties of young people living in the drug-crazed and free-love days of the late 1960s. This exposure produced in me a kind of ravenous appetite for sexual con-quests. I became promiscuous. For me, sex was detached from love, and yet, I was desiring desperately to love and be loved. The lifestyle that resulted from my endless search was marked by drug and alcohol addiction, crime, and, ultimately, incarceration. When you mix pain, rejection, and instability together, the result is toxic. This pain resulted in me becoming a person who inflicted pain upon others: a hurt person hurting others.

It was there, at the dead end of Pain Place, that I came to know real love in the person of Jesus Christ. In the midst of despair, I encountered the God who had been searching for me and suffering with me since my childhood. This is often the way in which God makes use of our pain. In the words of C. S. Lewis, "God whispers to us in our pleasures, speaks in our conscience, but shouts in our pains."[6] For the first time in my life, I had ears to hear the voice of God shouting to me, "I am here, and I love you."

Not until years later, though, at a serendipitous encounter at the movie theatre had I ever dared speak to anyone—not even God—about being sexually molested for years by an older male cousin. I had never dealt with the deep pain caused by my parents' divorce. I had never processed the sense of rejection surrounding my conception and birth. I had never faced the devastation wrought in my life by my parents' serial adulteries. Now, in that theater, I could no longer hold it in. The dam broke. The tears flowed. A burst of angry, filthy language exploded from my broken heart. I felt like a vulnerable child again.

Our pain is often the result of decisions made by other people, especially family members who directly impact our lives. What can we do in these cases? Does the Bible offer any help in dealing with this pain?

The Story of Joseph

If you are like me, you probably have such a high view of Scripture, with its ancient stories and awesome characters, that you find it difficult to believe that the "people of the Book" were the same kind of people that we are—quite ordinary! The characters of the Bible were not supermen or superwomen untouched by the anger, resentment, and pain that can so easily typify our lives.

Do you remember the story of Joseph? Talk about a dysfunctional family! Joe's dad, Jacob, was a schemer from birth, basically "tripping up" his older brother by stealing his birthright from their blind dad with the help of his codependent mom, Rachel. The soap opera continues: Jacob fled from his home in fear of his life into the land of a distant relative (himself a swindler) and married two sisters—one he did not love and the other who could not give him a son. You can almost feel the tension in that household. Eventually, the Lord opened the barren womb of Rachel, and she gave birth to little Joey, followed later by Benjamin. These two boys became their dad's favorites, which did not go unnoticed by their ten older brothers.

While the sons of lackluster Leah worked hard tending the livestock, Joseph, very much his father's son, seemed to develop a head for numbers. He managed the business affairs of the family's large and prosperous estate, and as a token of his father's love and sign of his position, Joseph was given a tailor-made and dazzling "coat of many colors" (Gen. 37:3).[7] According to Chuck Swindoll, "This tunic was more than a simple gift from a loving father. It was a long-sleeved garment worn by the nobility of the day, a symbol of authority and favored position within the family."[8] Surely Joseph wore the coat with great pride upon every occasion, especially at family functions! "Check out my new coat, Judah!" Joseph may have quipped as he strutted past his sheep-scented sibling. He knew he was no ordinary Joe.

Joseph also had vivid dreams while he slept (echoing the experiences of his father, Jacob). One such dream, which begged interpretation, involved him serving as the source of sustenance for his family. He was actually the star of the show in his own dream (Gen. 37:5-8). Some visions are better left unshared. So, here he is: daddy's favorite, good-looking like his mom, strutting around in his new coat, and sharing his dream in which he is the savior of his family. You can imagine how this went over with his older brothers.

That was when, perhaps for the first time, Joseph began to experience real pain, which came in the form of betrayal, rage, and attempted murder at the hands of his own brothers. They finally had had enough of daddy's little dreamer. Their opportunity came when Jacob sent Joseph to check up on the family business. Upon seeing their little brother approaching, the wheels in their minds began spinning angrily, and there, danger met opportunity. Only Reuben's intervention kept them from murdering Joseph. Instead, they decided to throw him into a pit without food or water and let nature take its course. However, upon seeing a caravan of traders headed toward Egypt, they instead struck upon the idea of selling the dreamer. And thus Joseph, the once favored son of his father, became a slave, betrayed by his brothers. During the next decade of his life, his dream seemed to disappear.

Have you ever been hurt deeply by a family member, betrayed by a best friend, or abused by a parent? How do you handle such pain? Is it possible to become a victor instead of a victim? Is it possible to become better instead of bitter in the aftermath of such an experience?

The story of Joseph teaches us that such victory is possible. It is not automatic, and certainly not painless. Rather, it is a process guided by the sovereign hands of a loving Father, and it is meant for our good, and not for our evil. In the words of John Calvin,

> If Joseph had allowed his thoughts to dwell on the treachery of his brethren, he could never have recovered his brotherly affection for them; but when he considered the providence of God, he forgot the injury which they had done to him, and said: 'Ye thought evil against me, but God meant it for good, to bring to pass, as it is this day, to save much people alive. Now, therefore, fear ye not; I will nourish you and your little ones' (Gen. 45:8, 11, 19-21).[9]

The decision of Joseph's brothers to sell him into slavery was evil and never should have happened; it was not God's will. It was no doubt inspired by the enemy (Satan, the devil) and meant to bring an end to the people of God. However, clearly God wanted Joseph in Egypt. All of his God-given dreams could only come true there. However, God never causes evil in order to fulfill His will. Joseph's brothers made an immoral decision. It brought Joseph great pain, and yet God, in His providence, allowed it and even used it.[10] This is akin to what Paul states in Romans 8:28: "And we know that all things work together for good to those who love God, to those who are the called according to His purpose."

Upon careful examination of the life of Joseph, only the conclusion of the story makes the suffering he experienced meaningful. He suffered separation from the father who loved him, the rejection and brutality of his brothers, the hopelessness of being sold into slavery, the lying and retribution of Potiphar's wife, and the despair and isolation of prison. And yet, in the end, Joseph was a victor and not a victim—better and not bitter. What made the difference?

Lessons Learned

Throughout Joseph's trial, three key decisions enabled him to endure suffering without becoming pain's bitter casualty. First, he decided to remember. In spite of his circumstances, he remembered that he was the beloved son of his father. He remembered the dream God had given him, and he remembered that his family's survival depended on the fulfillment of that vision. As he prayed and meditated on the dream, it became clear that there was more at stake than his personal security. He remembered the stories told by his father, Jacob, about the faithfulness of his God. Even in his darkest days, God had not forgotten Joseph. Again, Swindoll encourages us: "The next time you feel forgotten, forsaken, or disillusioned, remember that there is one who is trustworthy, and He has not forsaken or forgotten you."[11]

Second, Joseph decided to forget. He even named his firstborn son "Manasseh," which means "making forgetful," declaring, "God has made me to forget all my toil and all my father's house" (Gen. 41:51). In choosing to forget, Joseph was not minimizing the trials he experienced, but he was refusing to drive down the road of life looking in the rearview mirror. In other words, in spite of the tremendous pain Joseph had endured, he was determined to move on with his life into the purposes of God. In fact, every time Joseph looked at Manasseh, he was reminded to forget!

Third, and most importantly, Joseph decided to forgive. In the most tender scene of the story, Joseph's brothers feared that after the death of their father he would exact revenge because of their past cruelty. They sent a messenger to remind

Joseph of their father's dying wish—that Joseph would "please forgive the trespasses of [his] brothers and their sin" (Gen. 50:16-17). Upon sensing their distress, Joseph wept and then uttered the famous words:

> 'Do not be afraid, for am I in the place of God? But as for you, you meant evil against me; but God meant it for good, in order to bring it about as it is this day, to save many people alive. Now, therefore, do not be afraid; I will provide for you and your little ones.' And he comforted them and spoke kindly to them (Gen. 50:19-21).

This, I feel, is the most important decision Joseph made. It is also the most important choice you must make on your journey toward healing the pain inflicted upon you by others. So, now let's talk about forgiveness.

The Power of Forgiveness

What is forgiveness, and what is involved in forgiving someone who has caused you pain? The Hebrew word translated "forgive" in the Joseph story literally means, "to take or lift away guilt." This term was used in a court setting in Israel. It referred to "the voluntary release of a person or thing over which one had legal or actual control."[12] In the New Testament, a common word translated "for-give" means "to let go" of something or someone.[13] This may remind you of the Academy Award-winning song, "Let it Go," from the Disney film, Frozen. I think this song was so popular because, like the sisters in the film, many of us need to "let go" of a lot of pain in our lives.

Joseph decided to let go of the hurt and anger caused by his brothers. This decision was hammered out through years of thinking and praying during his imprisonment. Perhaps Joseph's tendency was to play out in his mind his life's scenario, fantasizing about revenge and what exactly he would say or do if he ever laid eyes on his brothers again.

Soul-searching conversations with God undoubtedly softened Joseph's heart through the years. His focus turned to the purposes of God. The moment came when Joseph faced what Henry Blackaby has described as a "crisis of belief."[14] Would he use his God-given power to crush his now powerless brothers? Certainly, they had it coming; no one in the Egyptian court would have questioned his decision. Or would he fulfill the dream given to him long ago and become the savior of his people? The ripple effect of the decision to release his brothers from judgment went well beyond his lifetime and that of his children's children, to the Exodus, then on to Bethlehem, Calvary, Easter morning, and eventually to a movie theater in Texas where "Bye Bye Love" became "Bye Bye Bitterness."

Forgiving someone is both a single act and a lifelong process. Jesus described this as forgiving someone "seventy times seven" (Matt. 18:21-22). Forgiveness can rarely be based upon one's feelings. You may or may not feel like forgiving those who have caused you deep hurt; your feelings may seem to fluctuate. Surely as Roman soldiers cursed, spat upon, scourged, and crowned Jesus's sinless brow, the only thing He felt was pain. Nails driven through His hands and feet caused raw nerve endings to pulsate pain throughout His bleeding, broken body. He must have felt as though He were on fire. The physical pain was excruciating, but the emotional pain was equally real. Just days earlier, an adoring crowd welcomed Him with shouts of, "Hosanna! Blessed is He who comes in the name of the LORD" (Matt. 21:9). Now they were rejecting Him with cries of "Crucify" (Matt. 27:22). And yet Jesus prays, "Father, forgive them for they know not what they do" (Luke 23:24).

In my experience, often those who cause others great pain remain unaware of the long-term damage they are doing. I know this was true in the case of my parents. The old adage, "Hurt people hurt people" is more often true than not.

Yet Jesus was no victim! He did not die in defeat and bitterness. Jesus looked beyond the pain of the Cross to "the joy that was set before Him" (Heb. 12:2). This joy was the redemptive plan of God that could only come through His suffering, death, and resurrection. It was through suffering that Joseph was reconciled to his brothers, God was reconciled to the world, and I was reconciled to my family.[15]

If we cannot consistently forgive people by way of our emotions or feelings, then how can we ever release them and experience the freedom of sending the offense away? To repurpose a well-known book title, How Shall We Then Forgive?, we forgive by faith. We forgive by making a decision based on the truth of God's Word. We forgive in the power of God's Spirit, who lives within us. By an act of a Spirit-filled will, we choose to release our offender and cancel our debt against him or her. We do this by faith and not by feelings. We forgive as an act of obedience to our Lord's command, who taught us to pray: "forgive us our debts, as we forgive our debtors" (Matt. 6:12). The feelings, like the caboose of a train, may eventually come around once the engine of faith begins to move down the track of forgiveness. So, if you're just not "feeling it," then, start "faithing it."

What if I Don't Forgive?

The consequences of choosing not to forgive prove devastating. Physical illnesses often result from bitterness due to unforgiveness (Prov. 14:30). For years, I struggled with medically-diagnosed, debilitating migraine headaches that required treatment with expensive and harsh medications. After I forgave my mother, I began noticing that my headaches were becoming less frequent. Nowadays, they seldom occur.

For years, I sought in vain a deeper work of the Spirit upon my personal life and ministry in order to empower my evangelistic efforts. Such a baptism of power finally came not long after I released the pain of bitterness. As a result, not only do I continue to see multitudes of people around the world come to Christ for forgiveness, but I also see "Book of Acts" signs and wonders on a continual basis.[16]

Forgiveness has also impacted our family. After forgiving my parents, I became a more tender husband to Gina and a more loving father to our children: Sarah, Dillon, Joshua, and Madison. Generational strongholds that persisted for decades on both sides of my family have been broken.[17] Our family has become a walking billboard for the power of forgiveness!

Scripture speaks of several severe spiritual pitfalls awaiting those who refuse to forgive: unanswered prayer (Mark 11:25), demonic strongholds (Acts 8:20-23), grieving the Holy Spirit (Eph. 4:30-32), creating division and chaos in the church (2 Cor. 2:5-11), and perhaps even the loss of assurance of one's personal salvation (Matt. 6:14-15) can result from failing to forgive. In fact, a failure to forgive others is really a failure to understand what God has done for us through the Cross of Christ (Eph. 4:32). Forgiveness is serious business, friends!

Although I recognize the truth that Jesus is uniquely the Son of God in flesh and therefore no mere human could ever compare to Him in terms of His Person and Work, I also recognize that we are called to emulate Christ in redemptive suffering on behalf of others.[18] Paul spoke of "filling up what remains of the cup of Christ's suffering in my flesh" (Col.

1:24). Like Jesus, Joseph suffered because of his brothers. Like Jesus, Joseph's willingness to forgive his brothers provided their salvation. As with Jesus, God vindicated Joseph and gave him a position at the king's right hand. And like Jesus, Joseph prepared a place for his family to remain in his presence. [19]

One of the primary motives I have for forgiving those who have sinned against me (whether they did so knowingly or in ignorance) is the knowledge that if I, like Jesus, "endure the pain and despise the cross" (Heb. 12:1-2), God may well use my suffering to help that person come to himself and experience the joy of resurrection life under the reign of King Jesus.[20]

Conclusion

That day at the movie theater, I began a journey toward healing. I had been a Christian since my conversion as a troubled teenager. I had been in ministry for a decade. I was married and had small child-ren of my own. I loved God with all my heart, and yet I was carrying a load of pain-filled memories and consequent unforgiveness that threatened to crush me, my marriage, and my ministry. The decision to release the pain was the first step.

Shortly after this episode, I had a redemptive meeting with my mom. Like Joseph and his family, we wept together, confessed our sins, and experienced the healing of painful hurts. This ultimately led to my mom reaffirming her faith in Christ, leaving an abusive marriage, moving to Dallas, Texas, and helping Gina and me start a new church. She led countless numbers of people to Jesus over the next few years. Less than a decade after our meeting, my mom, at age sixty-one, was in the presence of Jesus. One day soon her body will be raised in glory! What made the difference in both of our pain-filled lives? It is the power of forgiveness!

This is not to say that all painful stories end well. I did not see my cousin since childhood, but I do know his tragic story. He became addicted to drugs, which led to violence, multiple arrests, mental illness, isolation, and an early death. As far as I know, he never accepted God's forgiveness through Christ, and I never had the chance to offer mine, though I have whispered it in the darkness hundreds of times since that day at the movie.

Periodically, I still deal with anger toward those who have hurt me, but I have found that "the just shall live by faith" (Hab. 2:4). The pain caused by others can lose its grip on your life only as you choose by faith to forgive. And God may well use your pain to speak to you and through you in powerful, life-altering ways.

But there is another, most sinister, and destructive source of pain. To this, we turn next.

Study Questions

Chapter 1: "When Others Cause You Pain"

1. What do you think is meant by the phrase, "forgiving is a single act and a life-long process?"
2. Explain the phrase, "Hurt people hurt people." Why do you think this to be true?
3. Read Genesis 45:7-8. What do you think Joseph meant by this?
4. What do you think Joseph's focus was while he was in the pit? What should be our focus when we are in pain?
5. How would you explain what is meant by, "Don't waste your pain."

6. What does it mean to forgive by faith?

2

When the Devil Causes You Pain (Pt. 1)

"Through it all, I've learned to trust in Jesus."

—Andraé Crouch

This Cannot Be Real

Nightmares are horrid things. For the past few months, Gina has been disturbed almost every night by vivid nightmares. As we discuss these disturbing dreams the following morning, we find solace that, though troubling, they are not real. The events have not been experienced in her waking time and space.

On June 24, 2002, however, I experienced every pastor's worst nightmare. It is as real to me as if it happened today. As painful as the memory remains, I feel compelled to share this tragic story.

Gina and I started Metro Church in 1993 with a small group of friends in Garland, a suburb of Dallas, Texas. The church exploded in growth, and by year nine we were seeing over 1,500 people attend the three services we conducted each Sunday. As is always true with any growing church, much of the excitement was generated by the hundreds of young people attending our services.

I knew most of them by name. Many had accepted Jesus as Savior and were baptized into our church family. I was thrilled to see them grow in their faith and love for the Lord. They were radical in their commitment to Jesus. They were the heart of Metro Church.

Our youth pastor, a young man named Mark Moore, was a combat veteran of the Desert Storm conflict. Our young people loved him, and so did I. He poured his life into these young Christians and taught them to live out their faith at home and among their class-mates at school.

Our youth group mirrored the city of Garland: a rich mix of cultures and ethnicities from up and down the socioeconomic scale. Some came from unchurched and tough backgrounds; a few were affluent. Many were leaders in their schools. Many had surrendered their lives to God's call to ministry. Others were still growing and developing as disciples, but each had found a place in the Lord and within the group. They were alive!

Summer was always packed with activities for the kids at Metro Church. Of course, the highlight of any summer was Student Camp. We worked hard each year to find the best camp possible and were thrilled when we booked a week at Student Life Camp housed at Louisiana Tech University in Ruston. Our kids were excited and so was the leadership of our church. We knew it would be a fabulous week for our students.

The Sunday before they left for camp, I did what we always did. When I finished preaching that morning, I said, "If you are going to camp in the morning, I want you to get up and come stand with me; we want to pray for you." Here they came: 150 teenagers teeming with excitement and anticipation, arms around each other as they came streaming down the aisles and stood with me at the front of the auditorium.

I asked the church family to join us in prayer. I recall the entire congregation eagerly walking forward, surrounding and laying hands on each student. Looking into their faces, I remember thinking, I have known many of these wonderful young people all their lives. Their parents received Jesus as Lord and Savior at our church. Many came to Jesus from a lifestyle characterized by drug and alcohol abuse. Marriages had been restored and families saved. I felt like all pastors feel: these were my kids.

"You are going to have the greatest time this week at camp," I said to them. "I'm coming down on Wednesday night to hang out and spend the night. I can't wait! It's going to be a great time. Some of you are going to stand up here next Sunday and tell what great things God did in your life. He's going to call some of you into the ministry. He's going to give some of you a renewed passion to live for Jesus."

As the congregation surrounded them, we laid hands on them and prayed. When we finished, we all said, "Amen," hugged each other, and went home fully confident of a great week ahead.

The Buses Are Here

Louisiana Tech University is about 250 miles east of Garland. It's a straight shot down I-20 through the small towns of beautiful east Texas. In order to ensure the safety of our kids, we chartered two buses for the trip from Discovery Tours, a national company with a great reputation. Early Monday morning, a new, brightly-colored bus drove onto our church parking lot at 6 a.m.—right on time. The second bus was de-layed by more than an hour. We would later learn that a scheduling problem had required Discovery Tours to contract with a second bus company who, in turn, contracted with yet another less reputable company. When the bus finally ar-rived, it was an older model and much less attractive. Our stu-dents would later recall dubbing it, "The Ghetto Bus."[21]

By 7 a.m., students were anxious to load up, hug their par-ents and younger siblings, say bye, and choose a bus to board. After a prayer for safety, they began loading the buses, enjoy-ing friends, music, and the doughnuts and orange juice that were prepared for them.

I stood beside parents and family members and waved as the buses pulled away from the campus. They were followed by a caravan of cars and leased vans filled with adult volun-teers. Several faithful church members had given up vacation time to serve as sponsors. They wanted to invest in the lives of these young people.

After their departure, I went home, tired from a long Sun-day and a very early Monday morning, hoping to get an hour of sleep before I restarted my day. As I opened the door of our home, the smell of coffee greeted me. Gina was up pre-paring for her day. Instead of going back to sleep, I poured myself a cup of coffee and sat down at the kitchen table. The Bible was lying there, so I reached across, picked it up, and began to read. My phone rang a few minutes after 9 a.m. This is when the nightmare began.

Is This Really Happening?

The phone call was from our youth pastor, Mark. The for-mer Marine was not an emotional kind of guy. When I heard the quiver in his voice, I could immediately tell that something had gone terribly wrong.

"Mark, are you O.K.?" I asked.

"Pastor, you've got to get here as quickly as you can."

I interrupted him, "Mark, what's going on? Tell me, what is happening?"

"Pastor, something terrible has happened," his voice breaking as he spoke through tears. "I—I don't know how to tell you this, Pastor. But one of the buses—the driver lost control—he drove it into the concrete support of the overpass outside of Canton. Oh Pastor—it's horrible. It looks like a war zone. One whole side of the bus has been torn off. Our kids—our kids, they are lying all over the side of the highway." And then he said, "Pastor, I'm not sure they're all going to make it."

This is every pastor's worst nightmare!

I tried to stay calm, but my heart was beating out of my chest. My spirit was crying out, "Lord Jesus, help us! Help us! Please, save our kids!"

I said to Mark, "Be calm; the Lord is with you. I'm so glad you are there with them. You will know what to do. Do what you can and have the sponsors care for the other kids. I will be there as soon as I can. I'm praying!"

I immediately called my Associate Pastor, Guy Shafer, and said, "Please don't say anything. Please don't ask questions. I'm picking you up in ten minutes." I headed for the door, trying my best through tears to explain to Gina what I had just been told. Without changing clothes, combing my hair, or brushing my teeth, I grabbed my keys, ran to the car, and drove as quickly as I could toward the home of Pastor Guy. We left his home and began speeding down back roads until we got to Interstate 20.

As we drove, we were praying non-stop. The heavy traffic on I-20 was coming west as we headed east. The news stations were already carrying the story and giving the location. We listened on the radio to traffic reports on WBAP, warning those traveling east on I-20 that the road was closed at the Canton exit. One news report stated,

> There has been a terrible accident on I-20 at the Canton exit involving a bus carrying Dallas area teenagers to church camp. There are many injuries; some are very serious. Highway Patrol is advising that traffic is stopped in both directions on I-20 and are advising people to avoid the area. We'll keep you posted.

It became a national news story instantaneously.

Several miles before we reached the site of the wreck, traffic was stopped. I looked in the air. There were helicopters circling. The news media was gathering. I decided to go around the halted traffic, hoping to find a State Trooper who could take us to the scene of the accident. Finally, I reached a sheriff's deputy and identified myself. He embraced me and with tears in his eyes said, "Oh pastor, I'm so very sorry. Follow me and I'll take you to your kids." I'll always be grateful to the brave men and women in blue for the courtesy and compassion they demonstrated that day.

The deputy and a highway patrolman escorted us through the maze of traffic on I-20. At various points, other patrolmen and local policemen took over and brought us to the scene of the tragedy.

As we approached the site, I could smell diesel fuel. Then the bus came into full view. The impact of the crash was so strong that it literally split the bus and sheared back the metal from the driver's side halfway to the rear of the vehicle.

Mark was right. It *was* like a war zone. The wreckage was scattered across the highway and spilled into the median.

Pools of blood were everywhere. Our precious young people were lying across the grassy area of the highway. Cries of, "I want my momma" pierced the air. Broken bones and lacerated limbs caused screams of pain. Adults were bending over on the shoulder nauseated at the sights and sounds. Survivors sat speechless in a state of shock.

And then I saw the make-shift sheets pulled over the bodies of four teenagers.

Michael Freeman, Lindsay Kimmons, Michele Chaney, and Amanda Maxwell lay motionless beneath the shirts of grieving friends. I fell to my knees and groaned out in prayer for their families. "Lord Jesus, Lord Jesus, help these families. Help them, Lord!" That's all I could say.

It has taken almost twenty years to pray through and process what happened that hot summer day on a Texas highway, but I believe I'm beginning to see things a bit clearer now.

Study Questions

Chapter 2: "When the Devil Causes You Pain (Pt. 1)"

1. Does it help you when you read about the pain others have experienced? Why or why not?
2. In reading the testimony of the bus crash, what was Pastor Scott's initial response to the tragic news? Can you relate?

3

When the Devil Causes You Pain (Pt. 2)

"For the first time in your career you have tasted that wine which is the reward of all our labors—the anguish and be-wilderment of a human soul—and it's has gone to your head."

—Screwtape to Wormwood in *The Screwtape Letters*

An Enemy has Done This

In the aftermath of the accident, one of our Metro Church elders asked me if I felt the crash could have been caused by the devil. I immediately rebuffed his query. "The devil does not have that kind of power. If the devil caused the crash, why weren't all the kids killed? Besides, if the devil or his demons were responsible, then we could have stopped it."

At that time in my spiritual journey, I was a proponent of Calvinism, a theological system which prioritizes a robust view of the sovereign-ty of God above all His other attrib-utes.[22] By the term "sovereignty," Calvinists mean the meticulous control of God over all events.[23] In some extreme versions, evil itself is attributed to God, albeit in an indirect way.[24]

Due to my Calvinistic presuppositions, I concluded that for some mysterious reason, perhaps unknown or unknowable to us this side of eternity, God had allowed (or even caused) the crash for a higher purpose. The spontaneous revival that erupted at Metro in the weeks following the crash, resulting in hundreds of young people being converted, was thought to be the "purpose" behind the fatal accident.

I have since changed my mind.

Who Is the Devil?

The devil is a featured actor in the opening storyline of the biblical narrative. As Michael Green notes, "You simply cannot write him out of the human story and then imagine that the story is basically unchanged."[25] He appears in the early chapters of Genesis as a subtle serpent who deceives Eve by disparaging God's character and casting doubt on God's Word. The Bible closes with the judgment of "the devil that deceived them" (Rev. 20:9). From Genesis to Revelation, we are confronted with the reality that there exists a being who opposes the people and work of God.[26] Though the devil is often successful in this attempt, he will ultimately be "cast into the lake of fire ... tormented day and night forever and ever" (Rev. 20:10). But where did the devil come from? Does the Bible give us a glimpse into the devil's origin?

The Devil's Origin

Most conservative Bible scholars believe that the devil was originally created as an archangel. The word "arch" means "high." Although seven angels are named in Jewish and

Roman Catholic theology, the Bible mentions only three by name. Along with Michael and Gabriel, Lucifer (i.e., "the Shining One") is mentioned in Isaiah 14:14-17. About Lucifer, W. A. Criswell notes,

> In that creation of the angelic hosts of heaven, God also created the most perfect and beautiful and glorious of all of the angelic creatures. God created Lucifer, and made him the 'son of the morning,' the light-bearer, the leader of the angels of heaven, and the guardian of the throne of God Himself. He made him above all of the other creations in God's created heaven and earth. The beauty, the glory, the splendor, and the brilliance of Lucifer brought pride to his heart, and he envied God Himself.[27]

The passage describes the fall of Lucifer from heaven as a result of his pride and overreach. The word "I" is used five times in two verses, giving insight into the root problem of this beautiful creature. Lucifer had "I" problems! He *saw* himself as other than he was created to be. He said "yes" to that which God had said "no" to. His self-will resulted in his being cast down from heaven onto the earth. Jesus testified to this when He exclaimed, "I saw Satan fall like lightning from heaven" (Luke 10:18).

Satan's fall affected God's good world. Genesis 1:1 describes the original creation. This *ex nihilo* (i.e., out of nothing) act occurred sometime in the past, perhaps, as most scientists believe, billions of years ago. But something happened between the original creation of Genesis 1:1 and Genesis 1:2, the latter verse describing the earth as having "become without form and void, and darkness [covering] the face of the deep" (Gen. 1:2). Many scholars believe that "in the gap" between the first and second verses, the devil and his angels fell and turned the original creation into something dark and deformed. Among these scholars is Gregory Boyd, who writes,

> Genesis 1:2 can arguably be translated, 'Now the earth became [or had become] formless and empty.' It is significant to note also that the terms used to describe the earth in verse 2 ... are almost always used pejoratively. Indeed, the only other time this exact phrase is in reference to the state of the world ... [occurs] after God's judgement ... so too we should recall that 'the deep' always had a sinister connotation in ancient Near Eastern thought.[28]

Another important passage giving insight into the devil's origin is Ezekiel 28. Going beyond the historical personage of the King of Tyre, Ezekiel addresses the spiritual being who is supplying the king with power to accomplish his evil intentions toward the nations. The being is said to have been "in Eden, the Garden of God" (Ezek. 28:13). Certainly, this could not describe any earthly Near Eastern monarch! Based on this text, many scholars believe that Lucifer was involved with the worship of God in heaven. Perhaps he was the primary worship leader. Musical instruments were a part of his very being. This has led interpreters to believe that Satan often uses music as a part of his arsenal to attack and deceive God's image-bearers.[29] The devil perverts God's good gifts in order to lead people astray. There is always a soundtrack to the evil of a generation. As missiologist William Langley explains,

> Lucifer was not only beautiful in sight, he was also beautiful in sound. 'The workmanship of your timbrels and pipes was prepared for you on the day you were created.' This scripture seems to indicate that the purpose for which Lucifer was created was that of glorifying God and even leading the angelic creation in worship. Yet, in his jealousy of God, rather than giving worship, he desired to be worshiped. To that end, he does all he can to hinder believers from

focusing on God in true worship today. His goal is to direct believers away from God so that their worship is either misdirected or nonexistent.[30]

Satan's pride of place and diabolical desire to supersede God as the Supreme Being led him to form a *coup d'état*. One-third of the angels under his direct command attempted to dethrone God (Rev. 12:4). Their attempt failed, and "that old serpent, called the Devil and Satan, which deceived the whole world: he was cast out with him" (Rev. 12:9).

So, who is responsible for the existence of Satan? Did God make the devil? The answer is a resounding, "No!" God created a beautiful, worshipful angelic being named Lucifer. Lucifer created the devil by saying "yes" to God's "no" and "no" to God's "yes." By an act of free will, Lucifer became Satan, and the angels became demons.

Since this pre-Edenic fall, Satan has had one primary purpose: he opposes God and all of God's creation, including the apex of creation, God's image-bearers (i.e., humankind). The devil does not hate humans as much as he hates God. If someone really wanted to hurt me, they would viciously attack my children. The same is true with Satan. Satan hates God and goes after those God loves supremely, His children. Jesus described the devil as a thief who comes to "steal, kill, and destroy" (John 10:10). Peter calls him a "roaring lion, seeking whom he may devour" (1 Pet. 5:8). The Revelation proclaims that "the devil has come down to you, having great wrath, because he knows that he has a short time" (Rev. 12:12). The earth is now the primary place of the devil's domain. He is called "the ruler of this world" (John 12:41), the "prince of the power of the air" (Eph. 2:2), the "god of this age" (2 Cor. 4:4), and his domain is called "the kingdom of darkness" (Col. 1:13).

Though Satan has already been defeated by Christ, his kingdom has not yet been fully subdued. He remains the leader of a guerilla army bent on terrorizing God's people and creating casualties of war. Throughout Scripture, Satan has utilized people given over to his deception to destroy the lives of others. Cain murdered Abel. Pharaoh slaughtered the babies of the Hebrews. Haman moved against Mordecai and the Jews. Herod practiced genocide against newborns. The synagogue of the freedmen martyred Stephen. Judas betrayed Jesus. This pattern continues to the present day.

The devil plays for keeps. He has declared war on God and seeks to do as much damage as possible, including the taking of physical lives. I believe he won a battle that day on Interstate 20. Five precious people were killed, including the bus driver, Ernest Carter. As far as anyone knew, Ernest was not a believer in Jesus.

The Devil and Mr. Job

What is Satan's strategy to cause pain in the lives of God's children? How does he operate? One example of such activity is found in the oldest piece of literature in the Bible, the book of Job.[31]

Job was a man who loved God, his family, and righteousness. God blessed Job with immense wealth. He was a man of honor, and his reputation in the land where he lived was impeccable. Job's is the portrait of the blessed life. He was healthy, wealthy, and wise. And yet all of this changed in a single day.

Why do the righteous suffer? Why does God allow them to suffer? These are questions that philosophers and theologians have wrestled with for centuries. The technical term for such questions is *theodicy*, referring to "the realm of theology or philosophy devoted to the vindication of God's goodness and justice despite the existence of evil."[32] In dealing with skeptics, the question often arises, "If God is all-good and all-powerful, why do bad things happen?" Swarms of reporters were asking this question in the hours following the bus crash. It's the "Big Why."[33]

Traditionally, Christians have been reticent to give too much credit to the devil in our attempts at explaining the presence of evil and the pain that results. C. S. Lewis once quipped, "There are two equal and opposite errors into which our race can fall about the devils. One is to disbelieve in their existence. The other is to believe, and to feel an excessive and unhealthy interest in them."[34] Yet, much of the modern world simply laughs at the thought that an actual devil might actually exist. This attitude toward all things supernatural is changing rapidly, however, with the paradigm shift toward postmodernity, a worldview that tends to be more open to the reality of spiritual beings such as angels, demons, and Satan.[35]

Since the Reformation, many theologians have tended to attribute everything—including calamities—to the plans and purposes of a sovereign and omnipotent God. "Even Satan is God's devil" was Charles Spurgeon's answer to the problem of evil. In other words, God is ultimately in control and has a purpose for everything.

This was my mindset at the time of the crash.

When we examine the story of Job, however, we find that the adversary is responsible for the suffering that befell God's righteous servant. Satan destroys Job's property, kills his livestock, murders his children and servants, and inflicts Job's body with open, oozing sores. The devil even incites Job's wife to call on him to "curse God and die" (Job 2:9). The thief indeed came to kill, steal, and destroy! Job was caught in the middle of cosmic warfare between the legitimate King and a rebel leader called "the Satan." As in any war, casualties ensued.

The evil, suffering, and pain that engulfed Job's life, and which continue to ravage our world today, comes from the adversary—not from God.

The Bible teaches that Satan and the fallen angels under his command wage war on the saints. Jesus recognized the work of the devil in inflicting a woman with physical illness (Luke 13:16), sending a storm on the sea that threatened the lives of the disciples (Mark 4:39), causing a young man to be mentally ill (Matt. 17:15), and entering Judas (Luke 22:3), eventually driving him to commit suicide (Matt. 27:5). The devil is said to be responsible for afflicting Paul with a physical illness (2 Cor. 12:7) and putting believers in prison (Rev. 2:10).

The devil seeks willing participants for his evil schemes. Sometimes these people are oblivious to how they are being manipulated (2 Tim. 2:24). Other times, they cooperate willingly and anxiously (Acts 13:10). They are Satan's "useful idiots."

Drugs and alcohol are gateways for participation in the destructive activities of the devil. The Bible describes this as sorcery (Gal. 5:20). The word translated "witchcraft" or "sorcery" is the Greek word *pharmakeia*, from which we derive our word "pharmacist." In the ancient world, a sorcerer was a drug dealer. He served as the local witch doctor who knew how to brew mind-altering drugs that opened up the users to demonic possession. The devil then manipulated these people to commit various evil and often heinous deeds.

I believe this occurred in June 2002. Post-mortem toxicology reports revealed that Ernest Carter was under the influence of drugs and alcohol at the time of the accident. Perhaps unwittingly, he was being used by the devil to kill, steal, and destroy the lives of dozens of young people that day. His own life was among the fatalities. Satan found his useful idiot.

God did not cause the bus crash. God did not have a mysterious plan. God did not use Satan to accomplish a higher purpose. God was broken-hearted that day. God was with us on the highway, sharing our grief and pain. God looks like Jesus hanging on the Cross; standing, weeping at a funeral; crying out to Adam with a broken heart. God suffers alongside us.[36] The Spirit groans for the final victory over evil (Rom. 8:26).

Did some good come out of this tragedy? Yes. Hundreds of people came to Christ. Among these was Dallas-Fort Worth radio and television personality, Jody Dean. In his book, *Finding God in the Evening News*, Jody tells his story. During his coverage of the accident, Jody encountered a church building filled with people who were able to pray and trust God in the midst of their pain. Jody heard me pray that many people, including members of the media, would be touched and would come to Jesus:

> These people were stricken, totally devastated by their loss —and yet so connected to God that they were able to say, 'We don't understand, but we give thanks.' I am quite sure that before that moment I had scarcely known there is a God. I had learned a system of belief, but to believe is not the same thing as to know. My small difficulties paled before people going through unspeakable grief—people who thought first of God's blessing and the blessing of others. These people *knew*, and they passed it on. Many things have changed in my life since that day because of one simple prayer. I was the member of the media they had touched.[3717]

This is the goodness of God. This is the wisdom and love of God. God is able to use the evil brought about by the devil to display His grace, love, and compassion. In the end, love wins. But make no mistake: God does not cause moral or natural evil. In the words of Jesus, "An enemy has done it" (Matt. 13:28).

Job and His Friends

I'm sure we have all had well-meaning friends who have tried to enlighten us during painful times in our lives. I've had such friends. (They are often wrong but seldom in doubt!). Job was no exception. Job's friends had a theology that presupposed this: bad things don't happen to good people. His friends sought to help him make sense of the shambles that lay around him. They offered well-meaning counsel.

One of his friends suggested that Job must have had some sort of secret sin buried deep in his heart. In other words, Job's suffering would not have come without cause. He encouraged Job to come clean and repent (Job 11:6). According to Zophar, Job was actually getting *less* than he deserved. If Job would simply repent and get right with God, all of his troubles would vanish (vv. 14-16).

Another friend, Eliphaz, the oldest of the trio and the first to speak, had a "rigid theology that left little room for the grace of God."[38] Though Eliphaz was moderate in his approach to Job, the implications of his speech were clear: Job was obviously in the wrong. Job was failing the test God had given him. He need only admit this, and the Lord would heal him (Job. 4:17, 5:17). Eliphaz *knew* this was true because God had revealed it to him in a dream! Clearly, that settled the issue! Job's trial in his view was a means of chastening, and, therefore, should not be despised (v. 17).

A third friend, Bildad, sought to defend divine justice and implied that, since God could never do wrong, what Job was experiencing must be the result of sin in the lives of his children (Job 8:3-4). Yes, he went there! Job's children were clearly responsible for their own deaths. Talk about blaming the victims! Bildad kicked God's servant when he was down. Again, Warren Wiersbe helps us understand that "In a word, Bildad was a legalist. The man seemed to have no feeling for his hurting friend."[39]

What caused Job's friends to respond to him as they did? Wiersbe provides penetrating insight:

> Why would three men speak to their friend as these men spoke to Job? Why were they so angry? There is a hint of an answer in Job's words: 'Now you too have proved to be of no help; you see something dreadful and are afraid' (6:21 NIV). The three men were afraid that the same calamities would come to them! Therefore, they had to defend their basic premise that God rewards the righteous and punishes the wicked. As long as they were 'righteous,' nothing evil could happen to them in this life.[40]

It's no wonder Job declared, "Miserable comforters are you all" (Job 16:2) and "you are all physicians of no value" (13:4). Everything Job's friends communicated was, in a sense, true. Sometimes we experience pain because we are out of line with God's will for our lives. In the next chapter we will look more deeply into this issue. God is just, and therefore He must punish sin. Pain does often result from God's chastisement. We do often reap what we have sown. However, none of these diagnoses were applicable to this particular ailment.

When our friends and family members suffer, we must be careful and cautious in our counsel as well as proactive and persistent in our prayers. It is interesting to note that there is no record of Job's friends ever speaking directly to God on Job's behalf. The best thing Job's friends could have done would have been to speak less to him and more to God, engaging in spiritual warfare through prayer.

Learning from Job

So, what can we learn from the Job story about the pain caused by our adversary? I believe there are at least *three take-aways* from the story that will help us face the assaults of the enemy.

Lament

Job's complaint came from the depths of his pain and loss. Though he came close to cursing God and vindicating the adversary's original claim, he later repented in humility (Job 42:6). Job's response to his pain-filled episode is not the stuff of Christian television. Interviewing Job would have made for a very disappointing inter-view. He flashed no "Pepsodent Smile" and had no bumper sticker theology with which to reassure the audience that "Something Good is Going to Happen to You." He was definitely not living his "Best Life Now." Job's response was an honest and at times raw and bitter complaint.

Is this response appropriate? Is there a place in our theology for lament? Has the groan gone from our Christian experience only to be replaced with a glib, "Smile, God loves you"?

The devil's aim was to persuade Job to abandon his faith. It seems as if many skeptical questions walked down the corridor of Job's imagination. "Where is God? Why is He treating me like this? "Is He a God worthy of worship? Why doesn't He just go ahead and kill me? Why did He allow me to be born in the first place?"

The truth is, there are no quick and easy answers. This chapter is not entitled, "5 Steps to Overcoming a Deadly Bus Crash." God can handle our lament. He is big enough to listen to our complaints. He is much more of a patient, loving Father than an authoritarian dictator who brooks no resistance and tolerates no questioning of His sovereignty. Most of Job's angry dialogue was directed at his super-wise friends who purported to speak on God's behalf. His anger was not so much directed at God (though at times this was the case), but at those who sought to represent Him. After speaking with Job from the whirlwind, God had more rebuke and disgust for Eliphaz, Bildad, and Zophar than for His servant, Job.

During times of great loss and pain, it is perfectly normal and right to lament. Like Job, pour out your complaint to God (Job 7:11). Let it all out! Scream, shout, wail and, dare I say, ask God, "Why?!" You may never get the complete answer this side of eternity. In fact, you may never "understand it better by and by." But you will no doubt, like Job, receive something far better: *an audience with God.* You will be drawn closer into His presence than ever before. God dwells with those whose hearts are broken (Isa. 57:15) and promises to comfort those who mourn (Luke 6:21). You see, God knows what it feels like to lose someone you love. He lost His one unique son at the hands of an unjust empire. Jesus also knows pain. He wailed at the tomb of a close friend (John 11:35). In a Job-like cry of dereliction, he screamed, "My God, my God why have you forsaken me?" (Matt. 27:46). The Holy Spirit feels grief (Eph. 4:30). He groans out in pain (Rom. 8:26). The Triune God humbly grieves.[41]

Endure

The Apostle James exhorted his readers to faithfulness in the midst of suffering by reminding them of "the patience of Job" (Jas. 5:11). The word translated "patience" is *hypomone.* It means "to bear up under" a load of pressure without being crushed. Job "bore up" under some tremendous stressors. He bore up under the loss of his property and livestock, the loss of his children, grandchildren, and servants, and the ruination of his good name and health. He endured the ridicule and false accusations of men he thought of as friends and counselors. He patiently took the withering assault of a cruel, relentless adversary. He was plagued by his own nagging doubts about the character of God. And worse still, he endured what Martin Luther described as the *deus absconticus*: the seeming absence of God. Alone, body turned black because of the scorching sun, worm-infested skin oozing pus, Job held onto his integrity! It is easy to serve God on the mountaintops of "joy unspeakable and full of glory," but we do not stay there long. We, too, are called to faithful endurance.

The Christian life has been likened to a battleground and not a playground; a battleship and not a cruise ship. Paul encouraged Timothy, his son in the ministry, to "endure hardness as a good soldier" (2 Tim. 2:3). He spoke of "wrestling not with flesh and blood but with principalities, powers and the rulers of the darkness of this age" (Eph. 6:12). Job was unaware of the spiritual battle that raged around him. We are not. We are often tempted to go AWOL in the service of our Commander in Chief. We feel at times like turning away from the battle lines in a run for safety. In picturing the spiritual armor God provides for His troops, it sobers me to think that there is no provision for our backside! God's army doesn't know the signal for retreat. Our calling is to pick up the cross and endure to the end.

Swiss Psychologist, Paul Tournier, speaks of our tendency to retreat when he writes,

> We are nearly always longing for an easy religion, easy to understand and easy to follow; a religion that would allow us to escape from our miserable human condition; a religion in which contact with God spares

us all strife, all uncertainty, all suffering and all doubt; in short, a religion without the cross.[42]

In the midst of the devil's onslaught, Job endured. He did not renounce his faith or take his own life. He maintained his integrity. Although he never got an answer for the "Why" of his pain, he endured. He encountered God as he never had prior to his painful experience: *Deus absconticus* became *Deus revelatatus*![43]

I would like to think that just as Jesus prayed for Peter during the time of Peter's sifting (Luke 22:31-32), so the Eternal Word was interceding on behalf of Job, counteracting the onslaught of Satan.

Jesus also endured. Hebrews 12:2 says, "[He] who for the joy set before Him endured the cross." He died on a dark, pain-filled Friday, but Jesus knew Sunday was coming!

Hope

Several remarkable hope-filled passages are sprinkled throughout the Job story. Job believes there is an existence beyond this corrupted, temporary one (Job 14:14). He believes that after his death he will see God face to face (19:26). Commenting on this text, Matthew Henry writes:

> Job was taught of God to believe in a living Redeemer; to look for the resurrection of the dead, and the life of the world to come; he comforted himself with the expectation of these. Job was assured, that this Redeemer of sinners from the yoke of Satan and the condemnation of sin, was his Redeemer, and expected salvation through him; and that he was a living Redeemer, though not yet come in the flesh; and that at the last day he would appear as the Judge of the world, to raise the dead, and complete the redemption of his people.[44]

Job longs for a Mediator who could build a bridge between himself and the seemingly distant God (Job 9:32-33). In doing so, he anticipates the entrance of Christ into human history. Again, Matthew Henry comments elegantly, "Our Lord Jesus Christ is the blessed days-man, who has mediated between heaven and earth. The Gospel leaves no room for such a complaint as this. Job knew not how to address God with the confidence with which he was formerly want to approach him."[45]

Many Patristic exegetes recognized in Job a type of Christ and his innocent suffering and later vindication by God.[46]

Because God's enscripturated revelation is progressive, Job did not know in his day what we know in ours.[47] Job was victimized because a great cosmic battle was raging between God Almighty and a rebel usurper, called "the Satan." We can hope (and battle) with a great deal more knowledge than Job possessed. And knowledge is power! We are not ignorant of Satan's schemes (2 Cor. 2:11). We have been taught to pray, "Deliver us from the evil one" (Matt. 6:13). We are encouraged to "resist the devil and he will flee" (Jas. 4:7). We have been given authority on earth to "tread on scorpions" (Luke 10:19) and "pull down strongholds (2 Cor. 10:4). We have the promise that, "God will soon crush Satan under your feet" (Rom. 16:20). We are described as "more than conquerors" (Rom. 8:37) because "greater is he that is in you than he that is in the world" (1 John 4:4). We understand that "for this reason the Son of God was manifest that he might destroy the works of the Devil" (1 John 3:8). Most importantly, we know that through His resurrection, Jesus has "spoiled principalities and powers, triumphing over them in it" (Col. 2:15).

In the end, Job held true to his faith. In the words of John the Revelator, Job "overcame him [i.e., the Devil] by the word of his testimony ... loving not his life even to the death" (Rev. 12:11). The Lord restored to Job "twice as much as he had before" (Job 42:10). God vindicated his suffering servant. Job's "nightmare" became a faded memory (Job 7:14).

I have seen the same grace poured out on the lives of the parents whose children became casualties of war on that hot summer day in Texas. Through broken hearts and countless tears, they have endured, hope-filled, on their journey of faith. Holly Meehan, Amanda Maxwell's mom, posted these powerful words of hope on Facebook on the tenth anniversary of the crash,

> I praise God that my spirit is at peace. Trusting God has enabled me to forgive the bus driver, release the questions, and KNOW Amanda is loved and cared for. I better understand the verse in 1 Peter 4:12-13 today. "Dear friends, do not be surprised at the painful trial you are suffering, as though something strange were happening to you. But rejoice that you participate in the sufferings of Christ, so that you may be overjoyed when his glory is revealed." Rejoicing that I suffer is not it!!! It is finding that I can rejoice in the midst of the suffering that brings me to feel overjoyed. The pain has made me cling to God, for nothing makes sense or has hope without Him. Because of this, He has shown me how to live a full life now and to rejoice that the best is yet to come, when His glory is revealed. Then I will get to thank Jesus face to face for enabling Amanda and me to be together again.[48]

I, too, know I will see Amanda, Michael, Lindsay, and Michelle again. This is not some fantastical dream. This is "the victory that over-comes the world, even our faith" (1 John 5:4). This is the hope of God's Church, both militant and triumphant.

Study Questions

Chapter 3: "When the Devil Causes You Pain (Pt. 2)"

1. In a few words, describe what the Bible says about Lucifer according to Isaiah 14:12-17.

2. What word is used five times in verses 13 and 14 of Isaiah 14 that point to Lucifer's problem?

3. What do many theologians believe that Lucifer, the devil, was in charge of in heaven?

4. According to John 10:10a, what does our enemy desire to do to believers?

5. Job's three friends thought they had insight as to why Job was suffering. What does <u>Zophar</u> believe was the cause of Job's pain? <u>Eliphaz</u> "knew" the source of Job's troubles. What did he declare? What did <u>Bildad</u> say was the reason for Job's pain?

6. What is the best thing we can do for our friends and family when they are suffering?

7. What three things can we take away from Job's story that will help us fight our enemy? Please explain the meaning of these three terms.

4

When Pain Is
Self-Inflicted

"God it hurts to be human,
Without you, I'd be losing;
And someday, we'll face the music;
God it hurts, to be human."

—Pink

Lovers of Bible stories feel particularly fond of David, the humble shepherd boy who rose to serve as Israel's greatest king. Tracing his story through the pages of Scripture, you can't help but come to feel you know him personally. I see him: bushy-headed, medium height with a fair complexion, a musty odor of sheep and field wafting from his muscular frame. Full of life and all smiles, he is exuberant and particularly irritating to his seven older brothers.

David's story evokes images of adventure and excitement: giant-killer, legendary war hero lauded in popular song by throngs of adoring and grateful people, despised and hated by jealous Saul, vindicated by God and crowned Israel's king, successful in war, and passionate in worship. He is King David, a "man after God's own heart" (1 Sam. 13:14; Acts 13:22).

More than seventy Psalms are attributed to David. These represent the finest collections of poetry, wisdom, and theology available in all literature. David's giftedness as a warrior, leader, musician, and man of God is well documented in the Bible, in both the Old and New Testaments. Only Jesus is mentioned more in the Bible than David.

So, that is why—in light of all these accomplishments, attributes, and accolades—when we come to 2 Samuel 11 we hardly can stand to read of his great fall. I always brace myself for what's coming, though I have read the story hundreds of times—a story both saddening and maddening.

David's fall all begins with his taking a break from his duties as king. He is out of rhythm and out of sync with his regular routine. "But David remained at Jerusalem," we read in 2 Samuel 11:1. In other words, David has "checked out." Perhaps he feels as if he has done enough. After all, he has proven victorious in every battle he has ever waged. He deserves a break.

One dark night, restless and unable to sleep, David wanders out to his balcony for some fresh air. Is God calling him to pray or perhaps calling him to compose a new song for Israel's worship? Or maybe his conscience is bothering him? He thinks about his men and the sacrifices they are making to fight *his* battles and keep the fledgling nation safe from her enemies.

Suddenly, he sees her. What a beautiful woman! Who is she? *Whose* is she? A spark of lust has been ignited in David's soul. Unknown to him, this first undisciplined glance will soon kindle a fire that will eventually consume his own household.

Sin always operates this way: it fascinates then assassinates, thrills then kills. When sin is finished, it takes you further than you thought you would go, keeps you longer than you thought you would stay, and costs you more than you thought you would pay. David would soon discover the high cost of low living! James put it like this: "Then the lust, when it has conceived, bears sin; and the sin, when it is full grown, brings forth death" (Jas. 1:15). This is the devil's LSD: lust, sin, death!

The story that ensues rivals any current Hollywood drama or reality television program. Adultery, a failed cover-up, and, finally, murder, all flow from the headwaters of David's disobedience. Ever the great military strategist, he now uses his God-given gift to devise a plot to deceive and eventually destroy Uriah—now his enemy.

David has fallen. Temptation has overwhelmed him. Dietrich Bonhoeffer wisely strikes at the heart of the problem with which you and I, like David, wrestle:

> In our members there is a slumbering inclination toward desire, which is both sudden and fierce. With irresistible power, desire seizes mastery of the flesh. All at once a secret, smoldering fire is kindled. The flesh burns and is in flames. It makes no difference whether it is a sexual desire, or ambition, or vanity, or desire for revenge, our love of fame and power, or greed for money. ... At this moment God is quite unreal to us. [Remember those words.] He loses all reality, and only desire for the creature is real. The only reality is the devil. Satan does not here fill us with hatred of God, but with forgetfulness of God. ... The lust thus aroused envelopes the mind and will of a man in deepest darkness. The powers of clear discrimination and of decision are taken from us. The questions present themselves as, 'Is what the flesh desires really sin in this case?' And, 'Is it really not permitted me, yes, expected of me now, here in my particular situation to appease desire?' It is here that everything within

me rises up against the Word of God. ... Therefore the Bible teaches us in times of temptation in the flesh, there is one command: Flee! Flee fornication. Flee idolatry. Flee youthful lusts. Flee the lusts of the world. There is no resistance to Satan in lust other than flight. Every struggle against lust in one's own strength is doomed to failure.[49]

During the months that followed this debacle, David must have felt miserable. Matthew Henry writes concerning this self-inflicted dry season in the life of King David:

We may well suppose his comforts and the exercises of his graces suspended, and his communion with God interrupt-ed; during all that time, it is certain, he penned no psalms, his heart was out of tune, and his soul like a tree in winter, that has life in the root only.[50]

But God loves his chosen king too much to allow him to get away with sin. Nathan, a courageous prophet, shares with David a morality tale that infuriates the guilt-ridden king. Erupting in anger toward the fictitious plutocrat's selfish in-dulgence at the expense of a poor shepherd, David demands reparations for the offended party: "The rich man should die for his crime! Let him restore four-fold to the man whose little lamb he took as his own property" (2 Sam 12:6). David never lost his love for little lambs.

"You are the man!" the prophet thundered (2 Sam. 12:7). "David, *you*, the king whom God chose to bless above all oth-ers, *you* took the wife of your mighty man, Uriah. *You* have killed one of God's little lambs and taken his wife as your own! But God has seen it, and God is displeased with *you*!"

For the remainder of his life, David would feel the painful consequences of his personal failure. The "four-fold" judge-ment he pronounced upon the wealthy man in the prophet's parable was realized in his own family. "The sword will not depart from your household" (2 Sam. 12:10) rang in David's ears as he witnessed the death of his infant son; the rape of his daughter, Tamar, by her half-brother, Amnon; and Absalom's execution of Amnon as revenge for the atrocity. Through it all, David sat in silence as his household crumbled before his eyes.

Later, Absalom rebelled against his father in an attempt to usurp the kingdom for himself. This ended in David's beautiful and most beloved son dying in disgrace at the hands of the cruel general, Joab. David's broken-hearted lament is shared by every father whose son or daughter has died an untimely death: "O my son, Absalom! My son! My son, Absalom! Would to God that I had died for thee! O Absalom, my son, my son!" (2 Sam. 18:33).

After David's death, the hands of his son, Solomon, were bloodied by the murder of his half-brother, Adonijah. The four-fold judgment was indeed executed upon David's household: his infant son, Amnon, Absalom, and finally, Adonijah. All of them died tragically! Heaven only knows the potential for greatness that was sacrificed as the result of David's sin. Was it worth it, David? So much pain for so little gain? Never! F. B. Meyers' words drip with sorrow as he writes of David's needless suffering:

> This is the bitterest of all. To know that suffering need not have been. That it has resulted from indiscretion and inconsistency and neglect. That it is the harvest of one's own sowing. That the vulture which feeds on the vitals is the nestling of one's own rearing. Oh me, this is pain.[51]

This is the tragic testimony of all who have drifted into disobedience. I have experienced this painful truth firsthand.

Pain is Usually Self-Inflicted

Not all pain is caused by others; nor does all pain come from our adversary, Satan. I remain convinced that most of our pain comes into our lives as a result of our own sinful choices. Like David, I know about this kind of self-inflicted pain. For a brief period of time, I, too, lived outside the will of God. It was an excruciating experience I would like to relate to you. I do so in the hope that it will help you avoid making the same mistakes I made years ago. If you are now experiencing the painful consequences of disobedience, perhaps this chapter will help you find your way back into fellowship with your Heavenly Father.

My disobedience was not the result of a "blowout." It was more of a "slow leak." In my early twenties I served as the youth pastor at First Baptist Church in Sachse, Texas, then a tiny suburb in the Dallas-Fort Worth metroplex. Though God was blessing my minis-try to teenagers at the church, I had become embittered. I felt I was being underpaid and over-worked. In retrospect, the Lord was always faithful to meet my every need.

The truth is, I was exhausted. I was giving out nonstop. Run-away teenage boys were living with me in a tiny parsonage. Parents whose sons were out of control asked if I could help straighten them out. Many, having been kicked out of their church-going parents' homes, were now knocking on my door asking for help and a place to stay. For over a year, I "ate, slept, and breathed" young people. They became my life. I had no boundaries. It is all very clear to me now. I was burned out.

To complicate matters, I worked alongside a staff member who was struggling with his sexual orientation. (He would later be arrested for indecent exposure in a mall restroom). I was not mature enough at 23 to handle his struggle. Instead of

showing compassion, I inwardly passed judgment on him because of his struggle with sexual sin. (This would later come
back to haunt me). I became agitated by the thought that my
pastor, knowing of his struggle, kept him on staff and paid him
much more than I was making. The devil began using this to
sow seeds of discouragement and bitterness in the soil of my
weary soul. Satan was setting me up for a fall.

The church's Sunday morning attendance was made up of
around three hundred people, of which one hundred were
teenagers. When I arrived just a year earlier, there were
twenty young people in the youth group. The Lord had indeed
blessed my ministry, but the success had gone to my head. I
was filled with pride. Combine this with a feeling that I was
not as appreciated as I felt I should have been, and you can see
a disaster in the making!

That was when I met Danny Hayes. Danny was a guest
speaker at one of Criswell College's chapel services. I was attending the Southern Baptist college part-time while working
at the church. Often, the college would invite a minister to
preach and share a particular opportunity for ministry involvement with the student body. Danny moved from St.
Cloud, Florida to Texas in order to help the Baptist General
Convention of Texas with the Alpha Project: a bold initiative
on the part of the BGCT to plant 2,000 new churches by the
year 2000. Danny was assigned to pilot the project by planting
the first Alpha church in the Dallas area. His model was some-
what non-traditional, and up until that time in my ministry,
the traditional Baptist church was my only paradigm for doing
ministry. I was immediately drawn to his vision and the passion with which he conveyed his mission. I approached him
after his challenge to "dig ditches in the desert" and watch
God fill them (2 Kgs. 3:16). This was the beginning of a

relationship that lasted until his untimely death twenty years later.

Less than a year after I met Danny, he had left the BGCT and moved back to the central Florida city of St. Cloud in order to plant a new church. He asked me to follow him there and become the first full-time staff member, declaring, "Scott, you are the greatest youth pastor in America." This was music to my ears! Finally, someone recognized and appreciated my gifts and abilities!

I became the youth pastor at Osceola Church, a cutting-edge, slightly charismatic, elder-led, evangelistic Southern Baptist church. This relationship and experience became seminal for everything I would do for the rest of my local church ministry, and I feel grateful for all the wonderful things I learned during my brief time there.

There was, however, a dark side to the experience. I left my church in Texas and arrived in Florida burnt out and extremely lonely. It was the first time I had ever been away from my family or anything that felt familiar. Danny and I were very much alike in our temperament. In many ways, this was wonderful. He was a kind of big brother/father figure to me, but we were both *very* strong. His background was in youth ministry, having served as the director of Central Florida's Youth for Christ. Honestly, he knew how to do youth ministry far better than I. For the first time in my ministry, I felt I was the 'weak link' on the team.

I was very vulnerable in this place. Two or three weeks after moving to Florida, I began to sense that I had made a mistake. I had left my church family in Texas with a really bad attitude. Instead of staying in the place of God's blessing and trusting God for His provision, I stormed off like a child, drawn away by flattery and the promise of a greater opportunity. I approached Danny within weeks of arriving, telling him I had made a terrible mistake in moving to Florida. He *strongly* rebuked me, told me to grow up, to suck it up, to be a soldier, to "endure hardness" (2 Tim. 2:3). In my desperation, I called my former pastor, Billy Harris (an older grandfatherly figure), and asked him for my old job back as the youth pastor at First Baptist. He politely yet firmly answered, "No." I could sense in his tone a deep disappointment over my having left the church after serving there for such a short period of time.

After several months of being miserable and feeling like a failure in ministry, I sought for some sense of joy or comfort that could ease my pain and make life tolerable. Unfortunately, I searched for it in an inappropriate relationship with a single young woman in the church.

When you're out of God's will, you have no sense of God's peace. God's provision, His protection, and power seem elusive. Someone has said, "God is not obligated to pay for that which he has not ordered." You have to pay for that on your own. This is where I found myself in Florida. I had arrived touted as America's greatest youth pastor. I now found myself morally compromised and out of the will of God. To borrow an image from St. Augustine, I had pear-stained hands.[52] (St. Augustine recalls stealing pears for no other reason than simply to steal. He would later fall under great conviction as he would reflect on why he felt the need to steal.)

Another way of speaking about the will of God is to speak of seeking His kingdom first—submitting oneself to His rule and reign, no matter how difficult the task. This is the place of blessing. For me, this was at my church in Texas. Having sought my own will first, I found myself, like King David, in a backslidden condition.

When I began ministering to young people in Florida, I immediately sensed that something was missing. I employed the same strategies that had been so blessed in Texas. I worked hard. I prayed for God's blessing. But now there was no power. Like the young prophet of old, I was flailing away at trees without an axe head (2 Kgs. 6:1-7). Ministry became a chore instead of a joy. Soon, instead of a life-giving, God-honoring, and Spirit-empowered *ministry*, I settled for having a *job* at the church. I found myself going through the motions— drawing breath and drawing a paycheck, but my heart was not in it. How could it have been? I was double-minded and unstable. Philosopher Cornelius Plantinga describes this situation:

> Scriptural writers fear 'double-mindedness' not merely because it shows disloyalty and ingratitude but also because its perpetrators become its victim. Divided worship destroys worshipers. Divided love destroys lovers. To split the important longings and loyalties is to crack one's own foundations and to invite the crumbling and, finally, the disintegration of life itself. A divided house cannot stand.[53]

It is difficult to function effectively when life has become a dizzying merry-go-round. I felt engulfed in a fog. Nothing was clear anymore. Everything was a haze. I went on like this for weeks until I could take it no longer. The pain was too great. I went to Pastor Danny and confessed my sin. I met with the young woman and told her I could no longer go on living a double life. I was a broken young man yet relieved that the merry-go-round had finally come to a stop, albeit abrupt. It is always better to 'fess up' when you 'mess up' than to continue to live a lie.

Of course, I resigned my position. I publicly confessed to an inappropriate relationship, asked for the church's forgiveness, and agreed to a one-year supervised plan of spiritual and moral restoration. This included suspension from any involvement in public ministry. With the church's permission,

I decided to return home back to Texas, a journey of a thousand miles. I secured employment as a security guard (polyester suit and all), re-enrolled in college, and went back home to my church family. This time, it was not as "America's greatest youth pastor," but as a grateful and chastened church member—no longer the greatest anything!

The incidents I have described took place over thirty-five years ago now, but the memory still brings a sting to my soul and tears to my eyes. Though forgiven, I know that my sin produced a ripple effect. It always does. In the words of Plantinga, sin is "generative." Again, he writes, "After all, like virtue, sin is a dynamic and progressive phenomenon. Hence its familiar metaphors: sin is a plague that spreads by contagion or even by quasi genetic reproduction. It's a polluted river that keeps branching and rebranching into tributaries. It's a whole family of fertile and contentious parents, children and grandchildren. One more image, perhaps the biggest of the traditional ones: sin is "an evil tree" that yields "corrupt fruit."[54]

To this day, I am often haunted by the thought that parents had to explain to their sons and daughters the answer to the question, "Why did Pastor Scott have to leave our church?" I'm saddened knowing that the young lady with whom I was involved became embittered toward God, and, to my knowledge, never returned to her faith. I am angry with myself for having given an already skeptical world an excuse for mocking Christianity. I'm also often ashamed. I'm ashamed that I was not faithful to my wife, Gina, *before* meeting her. I'm embarrassed that my children have had to learn of this dark episode in their dad's life. In the words of David, "My sin is ever before me" (Ps. 51:3).

More than these often-crushing emotions, though, I feel grateful for the grace of God in my life. I feel humbled to know the depths of sin to which I am still capable of falling into, but for the mercy of God. After a year of probation from public ministry (during which time I grew personally as never before), God once again began to open miraculous doors of opportunity to serve. It started with going back on staff as the Evangelism Director at the church in Texas! (After six years in full-time evangelism, I returned to the church as senior pastor, replacing my pastor, Brother Billy). Then God began to open doors to preach large evangelistic outreaches involving thousands of young people in local churches, youth camps, and stadium crusades across America. It was during this time that I met, fell in love with, and married beautiful Gina. After thirty-two years, she is still the love of my life. The rest is, as they say, "His-Story!"

I've preached thousands of sermons in the past thirty-five years, (including several at the church back in Florida), and every time I step into the pulpit, I recognize that I stand there by the lovingkindness of a gracious Father. When we step outside of God's will for our lives, we receive the painful discipline of our Heavenly Father. He chastens us, not because He hates us, but because He loves us (Prov. 13:24). It is *very* painful, but it is *very* necessary.

Remember David? He sinned greatly, but he also repented. In a few moments we will look at Psalm 51 to feel the depth of this broken man's heart before God. Yet David continued to walk with his God. Here is what Paul said about David in a sermon in Acts 13:36: "For David, after he had served his own generation by the will of God, fell asleep and was laid unto his fathers." Not, "David the adulterer," but "David who served the Lord in his generation." (It has been observed that there is not one negative comment made concerning David in the New Testament). This is what I am doing: moving ahead into the promise of God for my life ... and so can you!

Like the Apostle Paul, I have nothing to glory in, except the Cross (Gal. 6:14). From God's point of view, all is forgiven and forgotten. I am forever a trophy of His grace!

The Road Back

How do you find your way back to the safety and security of God's will for your life? How can the peace, protection, provision, and power of God become real again? Is it too late for you? Have you gone too far, sinned too greatly, or been too bad to be received back into fellowship with God? Can you ever be restored?

It is important to understand that as your Father, God is actively committed to the relationship He has established with you through Christ. Though you and I may often fail to live up to our end of the deal, God is a faithful covenant partner. He keeps His promises. The Bible refers to this as His "loving kindness."[55] He is gracious and persistent in "completing that which He has begun in us" (Phil. 1:6). One aspect of His commitment involves His discipline. "He disciplines every son whom He receives" (Heb 12:6). This discipline is a vital part of the process of "conforming us to the image of His Son" (Rom. 8:29) and is spoken of as a part of His eternal purpose for us which has been "predestined before the foundation of the world" (Eph. 1:4).

God often uses courageous people to confront us with the sin and rebellion in our lives. All Christians are, in fact, exhorted to help one another bear the crushing weight of sin that we often see in a brother or sister's life (Gal. 6:1-2). This willingness to "speak the truth in love" (Eph. 4:15) to fellow members of the body of Christ is an act of compassion.

In the case of David, God sent a courageous spokesman named Nathan. David had approached Bathsheba; now

Nathan was approaching David. The eminent British biographer Alexander Whyte writes these words with regard to the courage, faithfulness, and skill of the prophet Nathan in confronting King David:

> Preaching is magnificent work if only we could get preachers like Nathan. If our preachers had only something of Nathan's courage, skill serpent-like wisdom, and evangelical instancy. ... We ministers must far more study Nathan's method, especially when we are sent to preach awakening sermons. Too much skill cannot be expended in laying down our approaches to the consciences of our people. Nathan's sword was within an inch of David's conscience before David knew that Nathan had a sword. One sudden thrust, and the king was at Nathan's feet. What a rebuke of our slovenly, unskillful, blundering work! When we go back to Nathan and David, we forget and forgive everything that had been evil in David. The only thing wanting to make that day in David's life perfect was that Nathan should have had to come to David. Now, what will make this the most perfect day in all your life will be this, if you will save the Lord and His prophet all that trouble, and be both the Lord and His prophet to yourself. Read Nathan's parable to yourself until you say, I am the man![56]

In the wake of Nathan's rebuke, David pens a painful song of lament. Psalm 51 acts as a roadmap for those seeking forgiveness *from* God and restoration *to* Him. The road back is marked by the signposts of brokenness, repentance, and restoration.

Brokenness

David recognizes that his sin has caused a painful breakup in his fellowship with God. He compares his condition to that of a broken bone that needs to be reset and healed (Ps. 51:8). As a former shepherd he remembers the many times in which he had used the rod to discipline a wayward lamb.[57] A particularly stubborn lamb would suffer the pain of a broken bone inflicted as corrective discipline by the rod of the loving shepherd. Now David was the wounded lamb crying out in pain from the depths of a "broken and contrite heart" (v. 17).

The way back into the will of God is marked by brokenness. Roy Hession describes this deep sorrow over sin as

> the first thing we must learn. ... Our wills must be broken to His will. To be broken is the beginning of revival. It is painful, it is humiliating, but it is the only way. ... This simply means that the hard unyielding self, which justifies itself, wants its own way, stands up for its rights, and seeks its own glory, at last bows its head to God's will, admits its wrong, gives up its way to Jesus, surrenders its rights and discards its own glory—that the Lord Jesus might have all and be all. In other words, it is dying to self and self attitudes. ... Being broken is both God's work and ours. He brings His pressure to bear, but we have to make the choice. ... this can be very costly, when we see all the yielding of rights and selfish interests that this will involve, and the confessions and restitutions that may sometimes be necessary.[58]

David's brokenness can be seen in the way in which he pleads with God for mercy. Notice that he does not ask for justice. Justice is the opposite of mercy. Justice is God giving us what we deserve. Justice is when God "rewards us according to our integrity" (Ps. 26:1). David had prayed this prayer in the past, but now his situation has changed. He is a broken man in need of God's mercy. Mercy is God withholding the judgment we are due.

I remember as a child playing 'the mercy game' with older, stronger boys. It was often a painful and humiliating experience. This is David: no longer the exalted king standing proud and tall, but a humbled and broken sinner lying in the dust, crying out for mercy. John Calvin, in describing the broken man, states the following:

> The man of broken spirit is one who has been emptied of all vain-glorious confidence, and brought to acknowledge that he is nothing. The contrite heart abjures the idea of merit, and has no dealings with God upon the principle of exchange. ... Where the spirit has been broken, on the other hand, and the heart has become contrite, through a felt sense of the anger of the Lord, a man is brought to genuine fear and self-loathing, with a deep conviction that of himself he can do or deserve nothing, and must be indebted unconditionally for salvation to Divine mercy.[59]

It is a painful reality check to realize the depths of sin to which we are all capable of sinking. "Let him who thinks he stands take heed lest he fall" (1 Cor. 10:12), is as true now as it was on the day Paul penned this penetrating caution. We are all one bad choice away from ruination. In the aftermath of my fall into sin, I remember reflecting on how it all happened so subtly. My prayer from that day till this is that I would live in a state of constant brokenness before God. Another word for this is humility. Humility is not thinking less of yourself. It is thinking of yourself *less* and thinking first of God and His kingdom, and of the good of others. I realize that this talk of brokenness runs counter to the prevailing ideas of the culture, perhaps even church culture. We have been too influenced by therapeutic models rooted in a shame-free, felt-need-driven philosophy. Sometimes it feels as if the worst thing a pastor can do nowadays is to confront our sin and failure before a holy God. Without a doubt, the twenty-first century American evangelical church has become a "non-prophet" corporation. In the words of Psychiatrist Karl Menninger, "Whatever Became of Sin?"[60]

From that day forward, David, like Jacob (and like me), would forever walk with a 'limp:' a reminder of his painful failure and the brokenness that followed. Only the broken person, though is a candidate for God's mercy. This is still a truism: "A broken and contrite heart, oh God, you will not despise" (Ps. 51:17).

Repentance

David's prayer in Psalm 51:13 is that as a result of his own contrition sinners would *turn* to God. The word translated *turn* is a Hebrew word connoting a change in direction; it usually ties to one's ethical or moral behavior.[61] David speaks here of his desire to turn away from his sin and to help others to do the same. God had used the prophet Nathan to bring about a change of mind within the king toward his sin. This change of mind resulted in a change of affections and will. Nathan, who had previously spoken to David on behalf of God concerning a covenant of blessing upon his dynasty (1 Sam. 7:4-17), now functions as a prosecuting attorney on behalf of his injured client, *Yahweh*. In response, David offers no defense. He pleads his guilt and throws himself upon the mercy of the court. The LORD is both the offended party as well as the presiding judge. David can find no fault with God's judgment (51:4). He knows that God is right, and he is wrong.

This is the heart of repentance. David makes no attempt to *justify* himself. After all, this type of lascivious behavior was common among ancient near eastern monarchs. Nathan could have been executed for merely confronting the king!

Nor did David *blame* Bathsheba, justifying his behavior with thoughts or statements like, "Why was she naked in full view of the king? Wasn't she trying to seduce me for her own advancement? She was not raped, after all. She was a willing participant."[62]

David could have simply *excused* his behavior by saying, "No one is perfect. We are all merely human: born in sin, conceived in iniquity. What did God expect? Why did He make me thus and then expect me not to eat forbidden fruit? How could any normal, red-blooded man resist such a gorgeous woman?"

But Scripture records David expressing none of these sentiments toward his sinful behavior. He comes clean. He repents. He humbly receives the prophet's rebuke. Matthew Henry describes the chastened disposition of those who truly repent: "But those who have been overtaken in any fault ought to reckon a faithful reproof the greatest kindness that can be done them and a wise reprover their best friend."[63]

This is the attitude of ones who experience genuine repentance: they feel they owe a great debt, and they long for the ledger to be 'blotted out.' They recognize their behavior as revolt, a "covenant violation on the part of a vassal against his suzerain [sovereign], and are therefore acts of rebellion of the gravest nature."[64] The heinous nature of sin requires that the offender be "washed," "cleansed," "purged," receive a "clean heart," and a "right spirit," and not be "cast away" from God's presence—all phrases from Psalm 51. This feeling of remorse, regret, and the desire for a radical change of direction characterizes a penitent person.

Repentance is the prodigal leaving the pigpen and returning to his father's house, Zaccheus coming down the sycamore tree and pledging to restore the money of everyone he has cheated, and Peter going somewhere alone and weeping bitterly after the rooster crowed. Repentance was a young man, broken by his sin, submitting himself to the discipline of his church and pastor and returning home to start anew.

Erasmus, the greatest of all Catholic Renaissance theologians, noted,

> The clemency of God is ready for all, not just those who have committed a few venial sins. For the Lord clearly promises, "Whosoever the sinner bewails his sins, I will not at all remember his iniquities. He does not make exception to any particular type of crime, nor to the number, nor the magnitude. Only repent of your sins and forgetfulness of all past crimes awaits you.[65]

The good news is that God is ready to receive and restore those who come to him in repentance.

Restoration

It is not enough for David to receive God's pardon. He desires restoration, but what is it that David wants restored? At this point he has not lost his relationship with the LORD. His salvation is based on God's *hesed*, that is, His covenant faithfulness. Yet, David has lost the "joy of his salvation" (Ps. 51:12) and perhaps, the *assurance* of being a part of God's covenant community. This sense of loss happens as a result of sin. While salvation is an objective reality, rooted in God's faithfulness and ability to "save to the uttermost those who come to him through faith in Christ" (Heb. 7:25), the subjective side, the feeling of assurance that all is well with our soul and God, can be lost. This is what David longs to experience again. He has lost his joy. He wants his fellowship with God restored.

He also realizes that the *Spirit* of God, which has rested upon him since his youth, has been grieved (Eph. 4:30-32). He has seen in his predecessor, King Saul, the devastating consequences of the Spirit being withdrawn and replaced by an evil spirit (1 Sam. 16:14-23). This happened as a direct consequence of Saul's self-will and rebellion. The fallen king realizes the dire situation in which he finds himself. David must choose: either his sins or his name will be "blotted out" (Exod. 32:32). David pleads with God: "Take not Thy Holy Spirit from me" (Ps. 51:11). He longs for God to uphold him with His free spirit (v. 12). His sin has bound him. He longs for the liberty that the Spirit brings (2 Cor. 3:17).

David is perhaps best known for his passionate *worship* of God. He was once unashamed to dance in the presence of God despite the disapproval of his wife (2 Sam. 6:14-23). He sings, shouts, lifts his hands, and offers sacrifices in the midst of the people of God. But this was before his great sin. For the past several months, his lips have become silent. His song is gone. He goes through the motions of offering animal sacrifices, but deep in his heart he knows that God is not pleased with mere ritual. David's conscience gnaws at him each evening during the time of Israel's prayers. He is guilty of the blood of Uriah. How can he sing of God's righteousness? He needs God to forgive and restore him in order that he might, "sing aloud" of God's righteousness and show forth His praise. Sin robs us of our ability to worship God "in spirit and truth" (John 4:24).

Unable to experience or respond to the presence of God in any meaningful way, David loses his passion to *tell others* of God's salvation. One of the first indications of a backslidden condition is that the overflow of our witness dries up. Sin acts as a dam which stops the life-giving reservoir of grace from flowing freely to those around us who thirst (John 7:37). I've discovered that it is easy to talk about what you really love. David, having lost his "first love" (Rev. 2:4) has no burden to see "sinners converted" to God (Ps. 51:3). Life itself has become burdensome (Ps. 32). The late D. T. Niles, British missionary to India, described evangelism as "one beggar who's found bread trying to show all the other beggars where the bread can be found."[66] David, having begged the bread of forgiveness, is now ready to share this blessing with others. David longs to be restored in order to restore lost sheep to the Shepherd's fold. Calvin comments regarding David's renewed passion for seeking the lost:

> Here he [David] speaks of the gratitude which he would feel should God answer his prayer and engages to show it by exerting himself in effecting the conversion of others by his example. Those who have been mercifully recovered from their falls will feel inflamed by the common law of charity to extend a helping hand to their brethren; and in general, such as are partakers of the grace of God are constrained by religious principle, and regard for the divine glory, to desire that others should be brought into the participation of it. The sanguine manner in which he expresses his expectation of converting others is not unworthy of our notice. We are too apt to conclude that our attempts at reclaiming the ungodly are vain and ineffectual and forget that God can crown them with success.[67]

Paul speaks of a similar phenomenon in 2 Corinthians 5:17-21:

> Therefore, if anyone is in Christ, he is a new creation; old things have passed away; behold, all things have become new. Now all things are of God, who has reconciled us to Himself through Jesus Christ, and has given us the ministry of reconciliation, that is, that God was in Christ reconciling the world to Himself, not imputing their trespasses to them, and has committed to us the word of reconciliation. Now then, we are ambassadors for Christ, as though God were pleading through us: we implore you on Christ's behalf, be reconciled to God. For He made Him who knew no sin to be sin for us, that we might become the righteousness of God in Him.

Those who have been renewed become effective at reconciling others to Christ. My own experience bears witness to God's ability to use broken people, especially in the area of evangelism. As a matter of fact, God may *only* use broken people. It is not our ability, but our availability that matters most. Just like the little boy's lunch, we must be broken and blessed before we can be used to feed the multitude. It is not our education, gifts, personality, physical appearance, or skill that God needs most. Certainly, He can use these attributes, but unless we bring these to the foot of the Cross and let them die, we can never know the power of His resurrection life flowing through us (Phil. 3:10).

By the grace of God, after being restored to the joy of my salvation, renewed in my worship, and refilled with God's Holy Spirit, I was released into a ministry of evangelism. I now preach the gospel with a broken heart, filled with compassion for a lost world. I'm thankful that God uses broken vessels.

Conclusion

There is an ancient art form in Japan that splendidly illustrates the theme of this chapter. Leading contemporary artist Makoto Fujimura describes the process of restoring the beauty and value of broken tea bowls.

> For centuries, there have been tea masters who perform the tea ceremony to visualize the invisible, as a spiritual and artistic practice. When precious tea bowls break, the families of tea masters will often keep the broken bowls for generations and later have them mended by artisans who use a lavish technique known as Kintsugi. Kintsugi masters mend tea bowls with Japan lacquer and gold. A bowl mended with gold is more valuable than the original tea bowl was before it broke.[68]

More valuable ... think about that. Self-inflicted pain brings brokenness into our lives, but God does not discard us. He mends us, piece by piece, until we are made new. Our value is enhanced in and through the process. Perhaps this was a part of the joy set before Jesus as He patiently endured the pain and shame of the Cross. It was as if the Cross was transparent, and Jesus could look through the agony of the Cross into the future where He saw a fallen, broken, and yet still valuable, young man who desperately needed to be mended with the gold of grace.

Study Questions

Chapter 4: "When Pain is Self-Inflicted"

1. After Jesus, who is mentioned more times in the Bible than any other person?
2. In Acts 13:22, how is David described?
3. What was David doing when his fall began? Why is this important to know?
4. What does the Bible tell us to do as believers when we are faced with lustful desires?
5. According to Proverbs 13:24 and Hebrews 12:6, what does our Heavenly Father do to those He loves?
6. It has been observed that there is not one negative comment made of David in the New Testament. Why do you think that is so?
7. What portion of Scripture is David's lament?
8. Name the three signposts of the "road back."
9. Define the terms *justice* and *mercy*. Explain the difference in the two.
10. In Psalm 51:12, what did David say he had lost?
11. Sin robs us of our ability to worship God in what way? (John 4:24)

12. Explain what is meant by "the gold of grace" as mentioned in the conclusion of chapter 4.

5

When Pain Is the Result of the Fall

"God is a concept by which we measure our pain."

—John Lennon

I hate cancer. It is hard for my teeth and tongue to form the word. The word "cancer" sticks in my throat. My mother suffered with cancer for six long years. Chemotherapy and radiation burned her insides. She endured constant nausea. Toward the end of her illness, she shook with fever and stayed drugged on morphine. Her beautiful hair fell out. She aged precipitously. Like all who approach death, she processed through the stages of denial, anger, bargaining, depression, acceptance, and, finally, hope.[69] She rediscovered her faith shortly before her diagnosis. Mom died at age sixty-one, only six years after she had begun to *really* live.

I have other dear friends who are suffering. One such friend is a young evangelical minister who has struggled with a strong same-sex attraction since adolescence. He risks ostracism from his peers at a conservative seminary. He longs to be 'normal'—thoroughly hetero-sexual like his classmates. He is suffering.

Another is a former student of mine who senses a call to evangelism. He has been wheelchair-bound since suffering a near fatal automobile accident as a teenager. He has lived disabled now for almost a decade. He struggles with depression. He wonders if he will ever make love to a wife. He asks if God will ever open doors for his ministry. He is a preacher who struggles to speak because of neuro-logical damage. He was once an all-star athlete. Now he needs assistance in the most private of life's necessities. He is in constant pain.

I recently lost a close friend. He was one of the brightest students I ever taught. After graduating with honors from a prestigious Bible college where he won awards in biblical Greek and theology, he decided to enter law school at the University of Texas at Austin. He graduated in the top ten percent of his class and received a clerkship with a federal judge. He then began showing signs of mental illness. He initially self-medicated with alcohol. This caused stress on his young marriage. His wife insisted that he see a doctor. He was diagnosed with bipolar disorder. After years of painful struggle, he lost his marriage and custody of his daughter. He was terminated from several positions at law firms. He became homeless for a time and was institutionalized. Finally, in desperation, he took his own life. I wept as I conducted his funeral. He was beautiful.

Suffering is real. Suffering is painful. John R. Stott states the problem succinctly:

> The fact of suffering undoubtedly constitutes the single greatest challenge to the Christian faith and has been in every generation. Its distribution and degree

appear to be entirely random and therefore unfair. Sensitive spirits ask if it can possibly be reconciled with God's justice and love.[70]

How can we make sense of such seemingly senseless suffering? We have discovered that pain is often caused by others, that it can be brought about by our Adversary, that it is much too often self-inflicted. But what about cancer? What about sexual orientation? Mental illness? Seemingly random car crashes? Does the Scripture offer us wisdom for such cases?

Grace, Groaning, and Glory

The eighth chapter of Paul's letter to the Romans is a Himalayan peak of inscripturated revelation. After trudging through the valley of despair and bemoaning, "O wretched man that I am! Who will deliver me from this body of death?" (Rom. 7:24), Paul begins an ascent in the Spirit up to the precipice of grace, and victoriously exults, "there is now no condemnation" (8:1-4), "no obligation" (vv. 5-17), "no frustration" (vv. 18-30), and "no separation" (vv. 31-39) for those "in Christ Jesus."[71] In other words, the Christian life is one of complete and absolute victory through the Spirit of the risen Christ. "We are more than conquerors through him who loved us," is Paul's climactic confession (v. 37).

And yet, there is suffering in our world. Christianity is not an escape from the painful problems and agonizing vicissitudes common to all. Prosperity gospel preachers say that because we are saved, we do not have to suffer. They get their deceptive message *out* of the Bible; they do not get it *in* or *from* the Bible! Consider the following passages:

"In this world you will have tribulation" (John 16:33).

"We must through many tribulations enter the kingdom of God" (Acts 14:22b).

"Yes, and all who live Godly shall suffer" (2 Tim. 3:12).

"Yet if anyone suffers as a Christian let him not be ashamed, but let him glorify God in this matter" (1 Pet. 4:16).

Being a believer does not mean you will never shed a mournful tear or have physical or financial problems. It does not mean that every family relationship will be wonderful, nor does it exempt you from mental illness. It does not mean everyone will embrace and celebrate the life you experience in Christ.

Christians can be separated from loved ones due to car wrecks, cancer, calamities, or COVID-19. Some believers have been forced into unemployment or bankruptcy due to the economic crisis of 2020. Faithful followers of Jesus have had to endure lifetime struggles with clinical depression. For many of our friends around the world, salvation through Christ means the loss of freedom, or even martyr-dom.

So, how is the believer to get through these difficult days? There is a note of triumph in what the apostle has to say here. Paul has thought about and prayed through the theme of suffering since his Damascus road conversion (Acts 9:16). He has experienced personal pain along the pathway of discipleship (2 Cor. 11:23-33), but he has come to a conclusion regarding suffering.

Two observations from Paul's Spirit-inspired reflection are note-worthy. First, he says, "I consider" (8:18). Paul uses a word that comes from the world of accounting, the Greek word *logízomai*. We get words like *logistics* and *logic* from that word. Paul says, "I've sat down, and I've thought about it, and I've come to a logical conclusion ... I've even written it down in a ledger!"

Second, he says, "I conclude." Paul states his conclusion: "the sufferings of this present time are not worthy to be compared to the glory which will be revealed in us" (Rom. 8:18). It's as if Paul wrote down the pros and cons of being a Christ follower and came to the overwhelming conclusion that it is worth it to live for Jesus.

In a similar passage, Paul encourages the church at Corinth to endure trials, reminding them,

> Our light affliction, which is but for a moment, works in us a far more exceeding and eternal weight of glory; While we look not at the things which are seen, but at the things which are not seen: for the things which are seen are temporary: but the things which are not seen are eternal (2 Cor. 4:17-18).

Paul is in no way minimizing human suffering. He knows firsthand the pain of life in its present state. However, when he compares the present to the glory God has in store for His children, it is like comparing a blue marble to the planet Earth or like comparing a T-ball team to the Texas Rangers (in most seasons!). In other words, they are not in the same ballpark.

Paul uses an interesting Greek word, *kairos,* to describe the time of human suffering here on earth (2 Cor. 4:18). He does not use the typical word for time, *chronos,* from which we get our term *chrono-logical. Chronos* is calendar time. It can be measured or 'clocked.' *Chronos* suffering is like the pain of pulling a tooth. It typically takes only a few minutes. We know this, and so we tell ourselves, "This will be over soon." *Kairos* time is different, though; it is more akin to a season. Paul uses the modifier "present," or, literally, "now," to further describe the season of painful human suffering. Paul says, "We are going to experience pain in this season. We're going to have it presently and persistently. So be ready to suffer—*now.*" And yet when Paul sat down to consider our present suffering in comparison with our future glory, he came to the conclusion that no matter how painful our 'right now' circumstances may be, they pale in significance in light of eternity. The end of our pain will be an *apocalypsis* (i.e., a glorious revealing) of who we *really* are: namely, the sons and daughters of God.

It is crucial to constantly keep this perspective in view. All of us suffer—some more severely than others. If we lose sight of eternity and focus only on the pain of our 'now' season, we will be tempted to become bitter and discouraged. It is also important to know with certainty that God uses our now-season suffering to conform us to the glorious image of His dear son, Jesus (Rom. 8:29). We grow through our pain—provided we choose to respond constructively. Earlier in his letter to the Romans, Paul reminds the church, "We glory in trials also; knowing that tests produce endurance; and endurance, character; and character, hope: and hope does not disappoint" (Rom. 5:3-5, translation mine). God has a purpose in our pain.

Robert Browning Hamilton expresses this truth in his, "Along the Road":

I walked a mile with Pleasure;

she chattered all the way;

but left me none the wiser

for all she had to say.

I walked a mile with Sorrow;

and ne'er a word said she,

but, oh, the things she taught me

when Sorrow walked with me.[72]

My football coach expressed the same truth (albeit with less eloquence), saying, "Scott, if there's no pain, there's no gain!" This is what Paul is saying: our pain has purpose.

The pain to which Paul refers is the result of the common suffering brought upon all creation as a result of the fall of humanity. Paul uses an intense word in Romans 8 to describe the response to this pain—the word *stenazomen*, used several times in verses 18-27, translated, "groan." Greek scholar, A. T. Robertson says that the word *stenazomen* refers to the "pains of childbirth."[73] Just as labor pains produce an agonizing groan from an expectant mother, so all of creation groans out in hopeful expectation that something better is soon to break forth. Believers join creation in this painful groan. Surprisingly, Paul says that God himself also participates in this hope-filled sigh.

The Groan of the Creation

The pain of the 'now' season is shared by all of creation (Rom. 8:19). Nothing and no one is exempted. By creation, Paul refers to all of the non-rational, impersonal, animate, and inanimate aspects of creation that we have come to know. Whether we are referring to alligators or Alleghenies, bats or botany, cats or cauliflower, dogs or dandelions, elephants or entire ecosystems, frogs or forests, giraffes or the grass under your feet, hyenas or the Himalayas, Paul includes the entire scope of the created order.

Where did creation's pain originate? Paul explains, "Creation was made subject to vanity [literally, frustration or emptiness], not willingly, but by reason of him who has subjected the same in hope" (Rom. 8:20). Creation was not made for, nor willingly choose to be, in the condition it is in today. Creation was subjected to futility. The word *futility* is the same term found in the Septuagint (the Greek translation of the Old Testament) as "emptiness" and is used some 100 times in the book of Ecclesiastes. It is typically translated "vanity," but it means "frustrated." It means that creation is unable to fulfill the purpose for which it was originally created. Creation was not brought into existence to cause hurricanes, earthquakes, or tornadoes.

I am from Wichita Falls, Texas. We call that region of north Texas and southern Oklahoma "Tornado Alley." Growing up, it seemed that every ten years or so a tornado would blow through and level the whole town! We would have to start all over. Creation was not made to produce tornadoes! There is a sense of frustration at work. Creation itself is groaning out to God for deliverance.

Where did this frustration and emptiness come from? Theologians often point to an episode in the biblical narrative called the Fall, which refers to the sin of our first parents, Adam and Eve. Created in God's image and given the mandate to "fill the earth and subdue it; and have dominion" (Gen. 1:28), humankind instead chose to go their own way. To paraphrase, God said, "I am making you like Me and putting you in charge. Your work is to steward the whole earth. I want to bless you and your children's children. All I'm asking in return is that you reciprocate my love through choosing to obey me."

But Adam and Eve were deceived by the serpent. They concluded that they could make it on their own. Perhaps they questioned the goodness of God. They said, "God, we are going to do our thing, and we don't really care what You have to say." God had previously warned them, "On the day you violate my commandment, you will die; and not only that, but everything over which you have been given oversight (the entire creation) will be cursed because of your rebellion" (Gen. 2:17).

Since the Fall, all of creation has been subjected by God to futility, emptiness, and disappointment. Adam and Eve's decision to disobey the Creator opened up a Pandora's box, so to speak, resulting in devastation, drought, disease, and death. From that season to the now-season, Paul says that creation "eagerly awaits" a change (Rom. 8:19). The word used describes someone "straining the neck, trying to look at something."[74] Paul personifies creation as standing on its tiptoes, sweat beading on its brow, straining its neck, anxiously awaiting the season of its deliverance. Creation is groaning out in pain.

Yet, notice that creation's groan is hopeful (Rom. 8:20). Dale Moody writes, concerning this hope:

> The age of glory belongs not to the past, as Stoic philosophers and many Christian theologians have thought, but to a future in which God's creation will share in the glory of God's children; and God's children will share in the glory of Christ.[75]

Indeed, God subjected creation to frustration, but not to be endured forever. The *new-season* is filled with hope.

Paul describes a cosmic redemption with which readers of the Hebrew Bible were quite familiar. For example, the Prophet Isaiah writes,

> The wilderness and the wasteland shall be glad for them, And the desert shall rejoice and blossom as the rose; It shall blossom abundantly and rejoice, even with joy and singing. The glory of Lebanon shall be given to it, the excellence of Carmel and Sharon. They shall see the glory of the Lord, the excellency of our God ... For waters shall burst forth in the wilderness, and streams in the desert. The parched ground shall become a pool, and the thirsty land springs of water; in the habitation of jackals, where each lay, There shall be grass with reeds and rushes ... no lion shall be there, nor shall any ravenous beast go up on it; it shall not be found there. But the redeemed shall walk there, and the ransomed of the Lord shall return, and

come to Zion with singing, with everlasting joy on their heads. They shall obtain joy and gladness, and sorrow and sighing shall flee away (Isa. 35:1-10).

I look forward to the day when wolves will lie down with lambs (Isa. 11:6), when there will be peace and tranquility between the nations (2:4), and when the glory of God will cover all the earth as the waters cover the sea (Hab. 2:14). But that season has not yet come. In this now-season, creation continues to groan. In the now-season creation is "laboring with birth pains" (Rom. 8:22), groaning out because it has been subjected to futility, groaning because of corruption, disease, death, and decay.

At the same time, it is groaning out in anticipation! Paul says this groaning is not the rattle of death. It is, in fact, the hope-filled groan of life—the kind of groan that a woman experiences before she is getting ready to deliver her baby. Our oldest daughter, Sarah, recently gave birth to our second grand-child, a beautiful baby girl named Olivia. Sarah endured a painful time of labor. She groaned, but all the while she knew that, after the pain, would come the joy of birth. Hers was the hope-filled groan of a new season of life. This is the very way in which creation groans! Though it has been subjected to futility in this now-season, there will come a day when creation *itself* is delivered!

N.T. Wright, in speaking of the new creation, summarizes,

> If you happen to live at the sharp end of the corruption of creation—on an earthquake faultline, for instance, or by an active volcano--you may sense the awe of that futile power. Creation can sometimes appear like a caged buffalo: all that energy and it's not achieving anything. And, thinking of wild animals, what about that promise of the wolf and the lamb lying down together? Is that just a dream? No, says Paul. It isn't a dream. It's a promise. All these things are

signs that the world as it is, though still God's good creation, and pregnant with His power and glory is not at present the way it should be. ... Creation is waiting—on tiptoe with expectation, in fact—for the particular freedom it will enjoy when God gives to His children that glory, that wise rule and stewardship which was always intended for those who bear God's glorious image.[76]

Creation's ultimate hope is not in a reversal of climate change, genetically-engineered foodstuffs with which to feed a hungry world, the preservation of endangered species, or even a vaccine that will cure the novel coronavirus. Our hope far exceeds a return to the pre-fall Eden. Our ultimate hope is that *Jesus is coming again* and that in the *new-season* He will bring to all of creation a glorious rebirth (Matt. 19:28). So, get your hopes up! Lift up your eyes! Your redemption—and that of all creation—is drawing near! *The now-season will soon* give way to the *new-season!*

The Groan of the Christian

Paul, continuing in Romans 8, now turns his attention away from the groan of non-rational, sub-human creation to that of humankind in general and believers in Christ in particular. He says, "Not only they [creation], but we also ... groan" (v. 23). Humankind as *imago dei* is unique, separate, and distinct from animals and the rest of creation, and yet there is an organic connection. Evangelist and apologist Francis Schaeffer astutely observes that, on the one hand, humans are *nothing* like the rest of creation and *everything* like the Creator. Schaeffer ties this immaterial aspect of human nature to the "breath of God." On the other hand, insists Schaeffer, humans are *nothing* like God and *everything* like the rest of creation. This material aspect he ties to the "dust of the ground."[77] And so, humans, composite, personal, and infinitely valuable beings, join all creation and long for freedom from the curse of sin. Paul terms this "waiting for the adoption, the redemption of our bodies" (v. 23).

What does Paul mean by the word *adoption?* The word refers to the rights and privileges which are ours both in the *now-season* and in the *new-season.* We have already been adopted into God's forever family. Paul speaks of this "child-making" experience earlier in the chapter in relation to our initial entrance into the family of God (8:15-16). We have been "born again," and therefore are now the "children of God" (v. 16, 21). We have received the "Spirit of adoption" and cry, "Abba, Father," yet our adoption has not been fully realized. There is a "child-placing" experience to come. The unveiling of our true identity is yet before us.

The same is true with our redemption. We have been "purchased from the slave market" and freed by the blood of Jesus, and yet we groan in expectation of a fuller redemption. This is tied to our future physical transformation, which awaits the coming of the resurrected Jesus and the glorification of our bodies. Paul speaks vividly of this transformation in Philippians 3:20-21: "For our citizenship is in heaven; from where also we look for the Savior, the Lord Jesus Christ: Who shall change our vile body, that it might be fashioned like unto his glorious body."

Both our adoption and our redemption await fuller expression. Evangelicals have tended to focus on the *initial experience* of adoption and redemption, typically referring to this as "getting saved." If you were to ask me, "Scott, are you saved?" I would instantly reply,

> Oh yes, I'm saved! I got saved forty years ago in the Tarrant County jail in Fort Worth, Texas. I was born again. I was a drug addict, an alcoholic, and a criminal. I walked into the jail cell one person and walked out

completely different. Yes, hallelujah, I'm saved to the bone!

However, a fuller understanding of salvation would also include the present and future aspects. I'm also "being saved" every day. And I am looking forward to the Day when my salvation will be completed at the coming of the Lord (Titus 2:11-13). Therefore, salvation, properly understood, is a threefold event. I *was* saved from the penalty of sin (i.e., justification), I am *being* saved from the power of sin (i.e., sanctification), and I *will be* saved from the presence of sin (i.e., glorification).[78] It is this last phase of salvation with which Paul is concerned here and for which we groan as believers. Our groan is caused by the painful suffering we are forced to undergo in the *now-season*.

We all know what it is to groan. When she was eight years old, our daughter, Sarah, was struck by a car on the road in front of our home. The impact drove her headfirst into the asphalt road. I was called from a helicopter; the voice from the CareFlite pilot said, "Reverend Camp, there's been a terrible accident involving your daughter. We're en route to the hospital. You'd better get to Children's Hospital as fast as you can. We're not sure if she's going to make it." I know what it is to groan.

Our second son, Joshua, was born premature. He could not breathe. They took him from Gina's breast and placed him in an incubator. It looked like a little coffin. I put my hand on that plastic box and prayed as my newborn boy struggled for his life. I held my wife night after night for weeks as we groaned.

We groaned when our first-born son, Dillon, came and said, "Mom and Dad, I'm gay, and I'm not interested in being a Christian. I'm going to live my own life and I'm going to live it my way." He was thirteen at the time. For the next decade he lived a self-destructive life that took him through an eating disorder, drugs, arrests, and ultimately to the brink of suicide. We had to have him hospitalized. And what did we do? We groaned out to God.

As we age, our physical bodies begin to break down. At the time of this writing, I am approaching sixty. Can I confess to you that I am groaning a lot these days? I was an athlete in high school (the older I get, the greater I was!) and was offered a college scholarship to play football. Forty years later, my knees make me groan, my shoulder makes me groan, and my back makes me groan. When I am out on my walk, I can feel the groan. I have a saved spirit, and my soul is being saved, but my body is not saved yet! I eagerly await the time when Jesus comes back and completes that which He began in me (Phil. 1:6).

What gives believers such hope-filled assurance regarding our future? How do we know that what Paul is claiming is really true? Paul says our confidence is based on something, or better, Someone, who we have already received. He calls this indwelling "the firstfruits of the Spirit" (Rom. 8:23). According to Everett Harrison,

> The concept of 'firstfruits' is prominent in the OT, where the Israelites were expected to bring the first ripened elements of grain, fruit, etc., to the Lord as an offering (Ex. 23:19; Neh. 10:35). By doing so, the offeror acknowledged that all produce was the provision of God and was really his. Implicit also in the ritual was the assurance from the divine side that the general harvest to be enjoyed by the offeror would providentially follow.[79]

Paul is using this as an illustration of the presence of the Spirit in our lives. God has pledged His promise to bring a greater harvest in which all believers will have a part. This greater harvest is the resurrection of our physical bodies (1 Cor. 15:22).

When I was a lad, my great grandfather had a peach orchard. I waited expectantly every spring for the first ripe peach to appear on one of his trees. Some of you may have a peach tree growing on your property. It won't be long before you'll be able to walk out in your backyard and notice that the first peach has ripened. When it does, you're going to pick it, take a big bite, and let its juice run down your chin. And then you're going to smile. Do you know why? Because you know that it won't be long until the entire tree is loaded down with peaches! You can't see them yet, but you've tasted the firstfruit, and you know the rest of the harvest is on the way!

Likewise, God has promised that one day He will complete our adoption by redeeming the bodies of all of His children. Indeed, that is what we are looking for, groaning for, and hoping for. This is why we can endure all of the painful trials that come into our lives as people who inhabit a broken and fallen planet. Paul's hopeful groan is also recorded in 2 Corinthians 5:1-2; speaking poetically of the transformation of our physical bodies, he says,

> For we know that if our earthly house of this tabernacle were dissolved, we have a building of God, a house not made with hands, eternal in the heavens. For in this we *groan,* earnestly desiring to be clothed upon with our house which is from heaven (italics mine).

Paul says that we are groaning. This temporary tent we live in right now will one day be folded up and put away, and we will have a brand-new eternal dwelling.

For Paul, and for all who have read and believed these words, this promise produces a steadfast hope: "For we were saved in this hope, but hope that is seen is not hope; for why does one still hope for what he sees? But if we hope for what we do not see, we eagerly wait for it with perseverance" (Rom. 8:24-25). We who have trusted Christ have never seen Him with our physical eyes. Yet, He is more real to us than our own dear loved ones. We are saved *in* hope, not *by* hope. This is the heritage of all believers in every stage of salvation history. Again, Moody explains,

> As Abraham, confronted by death, believed the promise and hoped against hope, so the Christian, in the light of Christ's death and resurrection, rejoices in the hope of sharing the glory of God (5:2). His God is 'the God of hope' (15:13). He looks for what he does not yet see (2 Cor. 4:16-18; 5:7). God's children are waiting with God's creation (vv. 19, 23).[80]

One word of caution is appropriate: when confronted by the pain, suffering and evil of a fallen world, it is perfectly normal and natural for the Spirit-filled believer to groan. Jesus groaned (John 11:33). We will see shortly that the Spirit groans. Groaning is good. We have crossed a line, however, when we begin to grumble (Phil. 2:14), then growl (Isa. 59:11), then finally give up on God (Heb. 3:8-15). So, groan on until Jesus comes!

The Groan of the Comforter

"Likewise the Spirit also helps in our weaknesses" (Rom. 8:26). That word *sunantilambanetai* translated "helps" literally means "comes alongside and helps us pick up a load" that we are unable to bear because of our weakness.[81] When the struggles of life become too heavy for us, we do not have to carry them by ourselves. The Spirit comes and helps us in our weakness. We often do not know what to pray for, given our difficult circumstances. We know that we *should* pray, but when we drop to our knees, we don't know *what* to say. It is in that moment that the Spirit—dwelling within us, giving us the assurance of our adoptive status, and serving as the firstfruit of our promised redemption—begins to help us pray with "groans too deep for words" (v. 26).[82] What does Paul mean by this enigmatic expression? New Testament scholar, Gordon Fee, in commenting on Romans 8:26, offers the following explanation:

> Several matters therefore, join to suggest that Origen probably had it right, in understanding these sentences as a whole and this phrase in particular to refer to a kind of private ('to oneself') praying in tongues that Paul speaks about as a part of his resolution of the practice of uninterpreted tongues in the worshipping community in Corinth. ... The present sentences, in fact, correspond remarkably with what Paul elsewhere calls, 'praying with/in the Spirit' (1 Cor. 14:14-15; Eph. 6:18). The correspondences occur at two crucial points: (a) the Spirit is the subject of the verb 'interceding,' that is, the Spirit himself is seen as praying from within us and (b) the persons involved do not understand what the Spirit is saying—or not saying, as the case may be.[83]

I bear witness that in my deepest seasons of pain, when I have difficulty in knowing how or what to pray, the Holy Spirit has gifted me with the beautiful language of Heaven.[84] Jack Hayford testifies to similar experiences when he writes,

> Do you have winter seasons of your soul? Of course, we all do! To mind come the number of times my situation has been snowed in or frozen over by sudden or accumulated pressures of trials. Do you understand exactly what I mean when I confess, 'Sometimes I don't feel like praying at all, and other times, though I do pray, it seems like nothing is happening—nothing but *nothing*'? ... But the apostle Paul writes of a sure-fire connection between two spirits, between the redeemed human spirit and the Living Father, our

Eternal Creator Himself. An assurance is wrapped up in the text above: When words fail and the soul seems chilled, there's a hot line to heaven that goes directly to the throne, a channel of holy commerce that never freezes over, whatever the conditions on our side of things! Let's allow the Holy Spirit to assist us in praying beyond our sensed limits of such moments. The simple statement of the Word is this: When I pray in tongues, I'm talking to God. Period! Whatever else anyone may say about the enjoyment of spiritual language, this is the Bible's bottom line. Tongues are connected to heaven's throne; that's all there is to it.[85]

When our children's lives were endangered, frankly, I was at a loss to know how to pray. I was overwhelmed with grief, pain, and frustration. It was then that the Spirit interceded with "groanings too deep for words" (Rom. 8:26). Praying "with my spirit and my understanding" (1 Cor. 14:14-15), was the means whereby the powerful hands of God were moved to heal and restore our children. They are all three alive and well, serving the purposes of God with their gifts and talents.

Groaning Gives Way to Glory

Ultimately, it is the Cross, that symbol of grace, which assures us of God's victory over all that causes our groan. Jesus is crowned king of the new creation on the Cross, but what a strange diadem he wears. "When they had twisted a crown of *thorns,* they put it on His head" (Matt. 27:29) (italics mine). Why thorns? Charles Spurgeon eloquently explains,

> The coronation of Christ with thorns was symbolical, and had great meaning in it, for, first, it was to Him a triumphal crown. Christ had fought with sin from the day He first stood foot to foot with it in the wilderness up to the time when He entered Pilate's hall, and He had conquered it. As a witness that He had gained the victory, behold sin's crown seized as a trophy! What was the crown of sin? Thorns. These sprang

from the curse. 'Thorns and thistles shall it bring forth to thee,' was the coronation of sin, and now Christ has taken away its crown, and put it on His own head. He has spoiled sin of its richest regalia, and He wears it Himself. Glorious champion, all hail![86]

On the Cross, Jesus bore on His sinless brow the curse of all humanity. God chooses not to destroy evil, pain, and suffering by *fiat*. Instead, through the Cross, God in Christ defeats all that is affected by the curse. Again, John Stott asserts,

> We have to learn to climb the hill called Calvary, and from that vantage-ground survey all of life's tragedies. The cross does not solve the problem of suffering, but it supplies the essential perspective from which to look at it. Since God has demonstrated his holy love and loving justice in a historical event (the cross), no other historical event (whether personal or global) can override or disprove it. This must surely be why the scroll (the book of history and destiny) is now in the hands of the slain Lamb, and why only he is worthy to break its seals, reveal its contents and control the flow of the future.[87]

The Comforter is groaning. The Christian is groaning. The creation is groaning. But the day is coming when our groaning will give way to glory. My young preacher friend will be rewarded greatly for his self-control. The broken limbs of the aspiring evangelist will be healed, and his beautiful feet will dance with joy. Because of God's grace, both my lawyer friend and my mother are experiencing a taste of God's glory that they never realized on earth. Yet, even in their present state, there is more to come. For all who have suffered and are now suffering, there is more to come.

Study Questions

Chapter 5: "When Pain is the Result of the Fall"

1. What does the Greek word *Kairos* mean in 2 Corinthians 4:18 in reference to our human suffering on earth?

2. This chapter refers to pain in two seasons. What are they?

3. Creation itself is groaning for God's deliverance. What episode in history caused this groaning?

4. Salvation is a three-fold event. Please name and explain.

5. Groaning is good, but we have crossed a line when we begin to do what? (Three answers all beginning with the letter G)

6. So for now the Comforter is groaning, the Christian is groaning, and Creation is groaning. One day our groaning will give way to what?

6

When Persecution Causes You Pain

"Called Didymas, preached the Gospel in Parthia and India, where exciting the rage of the pagan priests, he was martyred by being thrust through with a spear."

—*Foxe's Book of Martyrs* on the martyrdom of Thomas

Yaku Gamit was introduced as my driver for the week. Youthful and energetic, slight of build, and standing just over five feet, he quickly loaded my suitcases and those of our U.S.-based team into the rented SUV. Thus, began our journey into the distant city of Ahmedabad in the North Indian state of Gujarat. It was my first mission to India: the first leg of a five-week, seven-state preaching tour of the beautiful nation.

I had heard that Christians in Northern India faced persecution on a regular basis. They number less than 3 percent of the mostly Hindu region. In the weeks before my arrival, there had been several suspicious deaths among prominent Christian pastors. The news media reported the deaths as suicides. This aroused obvious suspicion within the tight knit Christian community.

As we journeyed, I noticed that Yaku was eager to engage in conversation (though his English was only slightly better than the few words of Gujarati I had managed to learn on the plane ride over). Thank God for our translator! One of our team members, Vivek Samuel, had known Yaku for years and asked him to share with us his testimony. Little did I know that my life was soon to be profoundly impacted by the man introduced as my driver.

A Modern-Day Apostle

Yaku was a new convert and recent Bible school graduate when the Spirit began impressing upon his heart the need for his village to hear the gospel and have a local church where people could gather for fellowship, worship, and discipleship. He began to openly share the good news with his family and friends. He was met with great resistance and threats of violence if he persisted in evangelizing. Undaunted, Yaku continued to share Jesus. The village elders responded with physical aggression.

A mob of radical Hindus—most of whom Yaku had known since childhood—encircled him and began mercilessly beating him. Cries for help went unheeded. They then poured gasoline on him and set him on fire while continuing to beat him with sticks. As he told the story, he lifted his shirt to show me the scars of his suffering. He was half-conscious as his assailants dragged him outside of the village to nearby railroad tracks. Using ropes, they tied him down and left him. They were expecting the train to finish him off. They wanted nothing to do with the strange new God about whom Yaku was preaching.

I interrupted the story with the question I'm sure you are asking now: "How did you escape? You're here now. Something must have happened. What was it?" By this time, everyone in the SUV was enthralled in Yaku's story. "Tell us what happened," I exclaimed.

Vivek chimed in, "Tell them, brother."

Yaku then smiled and explained, "The ropes just untied themselves and fell off. I stood up and was free."

My next question was, "Did you run to the next village to report this attempted murder?" Yaku smiled and told us that upon being freed (perhaps by an angel, although he never said so) he returned to his village and resumed preaching. The villagers, surprised to see him alive and well, concluded that their friend was a "holy man" to whom they should pay attention. This incident led to the founding of the first village church in that region. There are now over twenty such churches in various villages. Yaku pastors all of these churches. He rides a motorbike weekly to each congregation. He prays, teaches, preaches, administers the sacraments, and carries out evangelism.

My driver turned out to be a modern-day apostle, and like apostles in the New Testament, he has suffered greatly for the gospel. Suffering is not unique to believers living in India. According to The Voice of the Martyrs magazine, believers are now being systematically and violently persecuted in over sixty nations of the world.[88]

The first-century Church was well acquainted with the pain of being persecuted for the cause of Christ. Jesus addresses one church in particular, commending them and their "messenger," Polycarp, for their faithfulness under fire. This congregation resided in the ancient city of Smyrna in Asia Minor. Today we know the city as Izmir, Turkey.

The City of Smyrna

It may be helpful to take a look at the ancient city where the believers Jesus addresses in Revelation 2:8-11 lived. They were real people who lived under real persecution in a real city named Smyrna. Long before Rome began exerting her power throughout the known world, Smyrna was a prestigious Greek city-state. The city prided itself as the birthplace of the poet, Homer, the greatest writer of classical Greece. For hundreds of years it was an epicenter of learning, culture, sport and the worship of the pantheon. Gymnasiums and stadiums were built to host Olympic-like games where athletes competed for the *stephanos,* the winner's wreath or crown. Temples were erected in honor of Cybele, Aphrodite, Asclepios and Zeus.

And then, because of the hardships of war, Smyrna began to rapidly decline. For four hundred years, Smyrna ceased to be a city. It was reduced to a cluster of small villages. To all outward appearances, the city was dead. It remained dead until the Greek general, Alexander the Great, revived it. From that day forward, Smyrna was described as "the phoenix that had risen from the ashes by its own power."[89] Like Jesus, the city of Smyrna "became dead and came back alive" (Rev. 3:8). Every citizen, including the Christians, knew this history. Smyrnians loved their city. They were very patriotic. They were proud to say, "I'm from Smyrna."

By the time the exiled Apostle John wrote down his apocalyptic vision, the city of Smyrna was one of the great imperial cities of the Roman Empire. Because of the city's long loyalty to *dea Roma*, i.e., the goddess of Rome, it was chosen as the site at which a temple was erected to the godhead of Tiberius Caesar. The city was magnificently situated on a harbor. From a distance, Smyrna looked like a statue. Famed New

Testament scholar, William Barclay, describes the glory of
Smyrna and Mount Pagos.

> The setting of the city was equally beautiful. It began
> at the harbor; it traversed the narrow foothills; and
> then behind the city there arose the Pagos, a hill cov-
> ered with temples and noble buildings which were
> spoken of as 'The Crown of Smyrna.' A modern trav-
> eller describes it as a queenly city crowned with tow-
> ers.' Aristides likened Smyrna to a great statue with
> the feet in the sea; the middle parts in the plain and
> the foothills; and the head, crowned with great build-
> ings, on the Pagos behind. He called it "a flower of
> beauty such as the earth and sun had never showed to
> mankind."[90]

Because of land and sea trade routes, Smyrna had tremendous wealth, due primarily to the high rate of employment
among adult males. Trade guilds (similar to labor unions)
were common in the city, and each working man was expected to join and participate in the social customs of the
guild. These customs included obeisance to the Greco-Roman
gods, whose statues filled the gathering halls of the guilds. In
addition, once a year, all guild members were expected to bow
before an image of the emperor (in this case, Domitian), offer
a pinch of myrrh and utter the words, "*Caesar est Kurios*," or,
"Caesar is Lord." Domitian had only recently passed an ordi-
nance proclaiming himself *Deus et Dominus* (i.e., Lord and
God). Unless one was willing to do this, he could not be a
member of the trade guild. Those who were not members
could not get work. Without employment, one had no re-
sources and no status or standing in the wealthy city of
Smyrna. It would be easy to become destitute and therefore,
despised.

This was ancient Smyrna: the personification of all the wealth, excellence, might, intelligentsia, and religious devotion that Rome had to offer.

The Church at Smyrna

Throughout the history of the Church, the name Smyrna has been associated with suffering. Smyrna referred to a fragrant oil or incense that was produced by crushing a thorny bush. "Smyrna" sounds like "myrrh." The word is used three other times in the New Testament. It is used in Matthew's account of the wise men offering their gifts—gold, frankincense, and myrrh; it must have exuded a beautiful aroma, and yet, what a strange gift to bring to a child (Matt. 2:11). Then again in Mark's Gospel, as Jesus was hanging on the Cross in agony, soldiers offered Him a sedative, which He refused: wine mingled with myrrh to take the edge off His suffering (Mark 15:23). John's Gospel records that after the death of Christ, Nicodemus and Joseph of Arimathea asked the Roman officials for permission to bury the body of Jesus. They subsequently wrapped His body in one hundred pounds of aloe and myrrh (John 19:39). As a matter of fact, the city of Smyrna was well known for this herb used for embalming dead bodies in Egypt. They produced it and it made the city very wealthy.

In like manner, the church at Smyrna experienced several periods of crushing persecution. The church historian, Eusebius, writing in the second century AD, identifies twelve well-known Christians whose martyrdoms are linked to Smyrna.[91] Several prominent theologians have linked the church at Smyrna with an entire period of Early Church history (AD 64-313), characterized by ten intense periods of persecution carried out by ten Roman emperors.[92]

We are uncertain just how the church in Smyrna came to be. Most scholars are convinced that the church was the result of the outreach of Paul's three-year ministry in Ephesus (Acts 20:31). Smyrna is about thirty-five miles north of Ephesus and forms the second stop of a ringed postal route that circled that part of Asia Minor. At any rate, it was dangerous to be a Christian in the first century in the city of Smyrna. Jesus said the Church was experiencing *thlipsis*, translated variously as "tribulation" (NKJV) or "distress" (NET). The word literally means "pressure." W. A. Criswell describes *thlipsis* as

> pressure, like the execution of a man by placing a heavy boulder upon him. The weight of the great rock gradually crushes him to death. The word *'thlipsis'* has the picture of grinding millstones, the pressure of which, in heavy weight, grinds the wheat into flour. The word contains the idea of the pressure that forces the blood out of grapes. 'I know thy *thlipsis*—the pressure of persecution and sorrow and death.'[93]

The crushing that the believers in Smyrna experienced was due to their resistance to acquiesce to the expectations of a pagan society. They refused to honor the gods of the pantheon. They refused to say, "Caesar is Lord." They would not and could not compromise. All they would have had to do was to add this new God, Jesus, to the pantheon. Perhaps simply a small statue of Him hanging from their chariot or on the wall of their home along with all of the other gods was all the culture would require. All they would have had to do was to go along with the flow of the culture in Smyrna. All they would have had to do to make a good income for their family was to go to the guilds and offer sacrifices, pour out a libation offering, or offer a bull or goat on an altar to a pagan Greek god. All they would have had to do to have status in the city was to bow once a year to the image of the emperor. But that was the problem with these Christians. They had experienced Jesus Christ, the One Creator, God manifested in human flesh, and so they could not worship Zeus and Cybele and Aphrodite and Asclepios. They could not bow before the image of the emperor and say, "*Caesar est kyrios*." And so, they felt the pressure.

As a result, they became unemployable and then, financially destitute. Jesus said to them, "I know your poverty." Again, William Barclay gives us insight as to the extent of their poverty:

> In Greek there are two words for poverty. *Penia* describes the state of the man who is not wealthy and who, as the Greeks defined it, must satisfy his needs with his own hands. *Ptocheia* describes complete destitution. It has been put this way—*penia* describes the state of the man who has nothing superfluous; *ptocheia* describes the state of the man who has nothing at all.[94]

It is this second word, *ptocheia*, which Jesus used to describe the Smyrnian disciples. They were without the basic necessities of life: food, clothing and shelter.[95]

Pressured and impoverished, the church became the target of various slanderous attacks and the subject of numerous conspiracy theories. Rumors began to circulate about these Christians: "You know, those Christians, they're atheists. They won't acknowledge our gods." Others said, "You know, these Christians, they're wild sex addicts. I've heard that they gather together in homes and engage in 'festivals of love,' and you know, they're incestuous. They call each other "brother" and "sister" and greet each other with a "holy kiss." You know, I have heard the Christians are cannibals. When they get together in their meetings, they eat flesh and drink blood. And worst of all, I heard they are terrorists. They're insurrectionists. They say they have another King, so they refuse to honor Caesar. They say their King is going to make a glorious epiphany, an appearance with a great army, and that He's going to overthrow all the kingdoms of this world." And so, one by one, the Romans began to torture and imprison these Christians.

The source of these rumors was the Jewish community in Smyrna (Rev. 2:9). The Gospels and Acts portray the mounting tension between the followers of Jesus and certain portions of the Jewish community (Matt. 12:24-32; John 8:34, 41, 44; Acts 7:1-8:3; 9:1-9; 13:44-52; 14:1-7, 19; 17:5-9,13; 21:27-36). In addition, Paul seems to disqualify any person as being a true Jew who does not exhibit faith in Christ as messiah (Rom. 2:28-29; Gal. 3:26-29; 6:15-16).

After the fall of Jerusalem in AD 70, the rabbis began to distinguish themselves from those they saw as apostate Jews who had abandoned traditional Judaism in order to follow the "heretic," Jesus of Nazareth. A curse was pronounced on any Jew who abandoned the synagogue in order to join the new messianic movement: "May their names be forever blotted from the book of life." This is known in history as the *Birkat ha-Minim* or "curse of the heretics."[96] Tensions in Smyrna seemed to have been particularly high. A large and prosperous Jewish community had inhabited the area since the initial dispersion in 722 BC. As a result of their rejection of Jesus as the promised Messiah and their slander of His poor and persecuted people, Jesus labeled these Jews gathered for worship as the "synagogue of Satan." This is probably due to the fact that both the Jews and Satan were full of slander toward the people of God (Rev. 13:5-6). The division was deep and eventually turned violent. Eusebius blamed these Jews (along with the heathens of Smyrna) for the martyrdom of the elderly

Bishop of Smyrna, Polycarp, who was burned at the stake on February 23rd, AD 155.[97]

John Foxe elegantly summarized Eusebius's lengthy account of the Bishop's death:

> Polycarp, the venerable bishop of Smyrna, hearing that persons were seeking for him, escaped, but was discovered by a child. After feasting the guards who apprehended him, he desired an hour in prayer, which being allowed, he prayed with such fervency, that his guards repented that they had been instrumental in taking him. He was, however, taken before the proconsul, condemned, and burnt in the market place.
>
> The proconsul then urged him, saying, 'Swear and I will release thee;—reproach Christ.'
>
> Polycarp answered, 'Eighty and six years I have served him, and he never once wronged me; how then shall I blaspheme my King, Who hath saved me?' At the stake to which he was only tied, but not nailed as usual, as he assured them that he would stand immovable, the flames, on their kindling the fagots, encircled his body, like and arch, without touching him; and the executioner, on seeing this, was ordered to pierce him with a sword, when so great a quantity of blood flowed out as extinguished the fire. But his body, at the instigation of the enemies of the Gospel, *especially the Jews*, was ordered to be consumed in the pile, and the request of his friends, who wished to give it a Christian burial, rejected. They nevertheless collected his bones and as much of his remains as possible, and caused them to be decently interred.[98]

Thus the "angel" to whom the letter to Smyrna was originally addressed, departed to his Lord, Jesus.[99]

The Christ of Smyrna

Jesus promised His followers, including those in Smyrna, that He would be with them "to the end of the age" (Matt. 28:20). He addresses these believers in a similar manner as He does the other churches of Asia Minor. This letter is unique, however, in several ways that we will observe in this section. Initially, you will notice that this is the shortest of all the letters. It consists of only four verses, in which Jesus identifies himself, assures the Church of His providential and watchful care, tells them what is about to occur, and makes a promise concerning their ultimate reward.

Who He Is

First of all, Jesus identifies himself: "These things says the First and the Last." This is one of the clearest statements in the New Testament regarding the deity of Christ. It is a direct quotation from the Hebrew Bible. In Isaiah, Yahweh, the God of Israel claims to be "the first and the last" (Isa. 41:4; 44:6; 48:12). Jesus is claiming to be Israel's God. This is the confession of the Early Church: "Jesus is Lord." It is for this purpose that the true Israel of God could not possibly compromise by worshipping the pantheon or joining in the *cultus* of the Roman emperor. The city of Smyrna had oftentimes made this claim for itself: "We are *prote Asias*, first in Asia," they boasted, but Jesus claims this title for himself. He is the first and the last! The Smyrnian disciples could take great comfort in the fact that from A to Z, no matter what pain and pressure befell them, Jesus who is, in fact, God, was already there waiting. He is the "author and finisher" of their faith and ours!

Next, Jesus says He is, "the one who became dead and then came back to life" (Rev. 2:8). Isn't that powerful? Jesus says, "I'm like the city of Smyrna. I became dead, and by my own power, I came back alive." The construction in the Greek text is particularly helpful in giving this claim its full weight. Greek scholar A. T. Robertson comments

> *Which was dead* (hos egeneto nekros). Rather, 'who became dead' (second aorist middle indicative of ginomai) as in 1:18. *And lived again* (kai ezesen). First aorist (ingressive, came to life) active of zao (ho zon in 1:18). Emphasis on the resurrection of Christ.[100]

Simply put, Jesus passed through death as a kind of necessary but passing phase of His existence as the Son of God. Therefore, believers in Him need have no fear of death. The grave has been robbed of its power! Jesus has passed through as it were and has come out on the other side! He came back alive through the Resurrection. The church at Smyrna, as well as all those who are now suffering the *thlipsis* of living for Christ, have this encouragement from the living Christ: "I passed through death and began to live again. All is well!"

As mentioned earlier, this would have a special point of reference for the Smyrnians, both outside and inside the church. As J. Massyngberde Ford explains,

> The figures of speech in the prophecy are closely related to the history of the city. The speaker is the Son of Man. The epithet for the speaker is, 'the First and the Last' and 'who was dead and became alive.' The former contains a subtle allusion to the fact that Smyrna vied with Ephesus and Pergamum for the title, 'first in Asia,' (according to Ramsay); the Speaker insists that he is First. The latter may allude to the destruction of Smyrna by the Lydians: for three to four hundred years there was no city. The words of the ancients are, literally, that Smyrna was dead and yet lived. Our Speaker may indicate that the loses which Smyrna has sustained on the earthly level are compensated for by spiritual 'success.'[101]

And so, Jesus proclaims himself the exalted, reigning, Lord of every-thing. He is the one who has conquered death, passing through it and coming back to life again. As a result, the Smyrnian church has nothing to fear (Heb. 2:14-16).

What He Knows

Because Jesus is the resurrected and exalted Lord of all human history, nothing escapes His notice. He knows the *pressure* the Church is under. He knows the *poverty* that has resulted. Their painful plight has not escaped His purview. He is moved with compassion toward them. He has experienced the same pressure (Luke 22:44). Likewise, He has lived in poverty (2 Cor. 8:9). He has done so in order that He might faithfully fulfill His priestly role (Heb. 2:17-18). Having himself been slandered (John 8:41) and ultimately rejected by most of the Jewish leaders (19:15), He is able to bear the reproach of those who find themselves ostracized by their own family and friends (Heb. 13:12-13).

He also knows that *imprisonment* and death await these beloved disciples. Jesus says, "Don't be afraid of what's about to happen to you. Some of you are going to be put in prison for ten days." And, of course, we know from church history that there were ten distinct periods of persecution in the church from the time of the apostles until the Constantinian Settlement, the Edict of Milan in AD 313. Some scholars believe that "ten days" is an idiomatic phrase referring to a brief period of time (Gen. 24:55; Acts 25:6). Most likely, however, Jesus was referring to the immediate experience of His readers.

So, what did He mean by the expression, "ten days?" It was the custom in the Roman Empire, when a person was found guilty of a crime, to either execute the criminal immediately, exile the offender (as happened to John the Revelator), or confine the prisoner for "ten days," during which one's trial would be heard.[102] If found guilty, the person was typically released into the Coliseum, much to the glee of cheering crowds, eager to be entertained by the sight of blood. Many times, the emperor would wrap Christians in the skins of animals and release wild animals so that their bodies were gored or ripped, literally, from limb to limb. At other times, they would be made to battle to the death in the gladiatorial games. They were used as human torches, their bodies having been encased in hot wax, to light the imperial gardens during great festivals.

Unlike His strict warning to five of the seven churches addressed in the first two chapters of the Apocalypse, there is no word of rebuke to the church at Smyrna. There is no call to repentance. There is no word of correction. Jesus comforts, consoles, challenges and encourages His persecuted people.

What He Commands

Jesus commands His children to *not* fear death. Because Jesus, through His death and resurrection, defeated "him that had the power of death, that is, the devil" (Heb. 2:14), no believer in Christ need fear death. The greatest weapon the devil has is the fear of death (v. 15). Once we are freed from the torment of this fear by the love of God (1 Jn. 4:19), we become a powerful weapon in God's hand. A person who fears no one and nothing but God is a threat to Satan's kingdom. This is why the Early Church father, Tertullian, said, "The blood of martyrs is the seed of the church."[103] Nothing can stop the Christian (or the Church) who has overcome the spirit of fear (2 Tim. 1:7). Harvey Blaney, writing in the Wesleyan Bible Commentary summarizes,

> 'Fear not' calls to mind that God's people have always lived under a certain contingent jeopardy of their lives, and the common temptation has been to be

afraid—afraid of the forces which beset them and fearful lest they be unable to endure successfully. The great fear is always the fear of the unknown—anticipated events which cast their shadows before them and which may or may not take place.[104]

This first command is followed immediately by a second. The first is negative; the second, positive. Jesus commands His children, *do* be faithful unto death. Having prophesied the coming imprisonments and death instigated by the devil himself, Jesus now encourages His faithful followers to follow Him all the way to the point of death. This is in keeping with the call of Jesus to His earliest followers: "Take up the cross," was Jesus' invitation (Luke 9:23). I am reminded of Bonhoeffer's famous dictum, "When Christ bids a man, 'Follow me,' he bids him, 'Come and die.'"[105]

And die they did. They died by the hundreds throughout the Roman Empire. They died loving Jesus. They died laying down their lives for the gospel. This is what it cost for them to follow Jesus. This was the fate that Jesus knew awaited the suffering saints of Smyrna.

What He Promises

Now Jesus pledges His loyalty to those who have sealed their faithfulness in blood. Jesus has already looked beyond their temporal poverty and declared them to be rich (Rev. 2:9). Now He expounds upon the meaning of *plutosious* in the Kingdom. These pained, pressured, impoverished martyrs are destined to be plutocrats in the age to come.

First, Jesus says they will receive the *stephanos*, the winner's wreath, or crown of life. James, himself a martyr, mentions this "martyr's crown" (Jas. 1:12) that will be given to those who endure trials unto death. This image would be particularly vivid to Christians living in Smyrna. As William

Barclay writes, "First to the mind comes the victor's crown in the games. Smyrna had games which were famous all over Asia. As in the Olympic Games, the reward of the victorious athlete was the laurel crown."[106] Think of that! In the very colosseums in which the followers of Jesus died, others were given crowns to celebrate the greatness of their lives. Jesus promises that one day the tables will be turned!

Next, Jesus promises that those whose lives have been snuffed out as a result of discipleship will "not be hurt of the second death" (Rev. 2:11). Evangelist D. L. Moody once quipped, "If you're born twice, you'll only die once. But if you're only born once, you'll die twice."[107] The second death: what an unusual term. It is used again in the Revelation (20:6, 14; 21:8). To what does it refer? The Revelator himself explains the term that scholars refer to as an "epi exegetical" statement. Revelation 21:8 declares, "But the cowardly, unbelieving, abominable, murderers, sexually immoral, sorcerers, idolaters, and all liars shall have their part in the lake which burns with fire and brimstone, *which is the second death*." However fanciful or harsh this may sound to modern ears it remains a part of Jesus's promise to His people. It is also a warning to those rejecting Him. The crown consisting of eternal life is set in juxtaposition to a kind of death that knows no end. In the Christian tradition, we have typically referred to this conscious reality as hell. Jesus assures His faithful ones that they will never experience divine judgment. It will never be their portion. It cannot hurt them.

Please allow me to use my sanctified imagination in paraphrasing Jesus's words of promise to these suffering saints of Smyrna. I hear Him say something like, "Even though everyone in Smyrna said that you were a loser, that following me made you poor, and that you wouldn't worship the gods and 'go along to get along,' and so they took your physical life, now you'll be rewarded in front of the great cloud of witnesses in heaven and never be touched by death again! Well done, good and faithful servants of Smyrna!"

A New Smyrna Generation

We are currently witnessing a revival of political authoritarianism in the West.[108] If the twentieth century was characterized by the rise of democracy, increasing liberty, and human rights (including freedom of religion), the twenty-first century may well be the century of the autocratic strong man. Historically, this has always led to religious persecution. Authoritarian leaders tolerate no opposition. Anyone refusing to conform is in one way or another marginalized or eliminated. By and large, the West has been able to remain relatively free from violent religious persecution. There have been exceptions, even in the United States.

Early in the twentieth century, Pentecostals were often the targets of persecution. Because of their pacifism, many Pentecostal pastors, including the Church of God in Christ (COGIC) founder, Bishop Charles Mason, were imprisoned during the First World War.[109] At other times, Pentecostal evangelists and pastors were violently driven out of town for what was perceived as religious fanaticism. Personages and church buildings were burned to the ground. This was often linked to the integrated services held at the Azusa Street Mission and beyond.[110]

In the 1950s and 60s, church leaders—both black and white—propelled by their faith into the streets during the tumultuous days of the Civil Rights Movement were beaten, jailed, and murdered. This persecution climaxed in the martyrdom of the Rev. Dr. Martin Luther King, Jr. Few white Evangelicals have been willing to come to grips with the nature of this suffering. The fact is, it was the *black church* that was being persecuted in the streets of American towns and cities in the South.[111]

In the past several years, the news has been filled with shocking stories of deaths associated with religious persecution. Most of these were lone actors radicalized by hate groups. Chris Harper Mercer, a twenty-six-year-old man, shot and killed nine people and injured at least seven others. As details began to emerge of the terrifying experience of students and staff at the Umpqua Community College in Roseburg, Oregon, it became clear that the motive was at least, in part, religious persecution. Eyewitness survivors recalled,

> 'Are you a Christian?' he would ask his victims, and 'if you are a Christian then stand up' and they would stand up. He'd say 'because you are a Christian you're going to see God in about one second' and then he shot and killed them. And he kept going down the line doing this to people.[112]

On June 17, 2015, Pastor Clementa Pinckney and eight of his church members were martyred after a prayer meeting and Bible study at "Mother" Emanuel African Methodist Episcopal Church in Charles-ton, South Carolina. A twenty-one year old White Supremacist, Dylann Roof, attended the meeting and then opened fire. Dylann later admitted that he targeted the church because of its history and stature in the black community.[113]

The possibility of state sponsored persecution remains a real threat, however. As I write these words, John MacArthur, a prominent and fearless pastor of a Southern California megachurch, is being threatened by the state government for conducting services during the COVID-19 pandemic. Each Sunday, thousands of congregants are gathering at Grace Community Church to participate in the worship of Jesus

Christi.[114] My argument is not whether or not the pastor and leadership of the church have made a wise decision in choosing to gather during these difficult days. My argument is that the choice itself should be theirs to make. We are on a dangerous path toward persecution when the government begins to dictate to the church when, how often, and under what circumstances a sovereign church of the Lord Jesus Christ may gather.

These examples of pain and persecution pale, however, in comparison to the ways in which our brothers and sisters in the Majority World have in the past suffered—and are presently suffering—for their faith. However, I believe it would be naive to conclude that believers in the West, and especially those of us in the United States, will continue to be exempt from *real* persecution.

Prophetically, I want to tell you that I believe we will live to see the day where it will cost severely in this nation to be a Christian. The questions we must all begin to ask ourselves include:

Am I going to go along to get along?

Am I going bow my knee before a crass culture of materialism? Sexism? Hedonism?

Do I have the courage to stand against a growing authoritarianism in America and declare, "Jesus is Lord"?

Will I bow my knee at the altar of religious pluralism that says, "It doesn't matter if you worship Jesus or Mohammed or Buddha or Krishna! It doesn't matter! They're all the same!"

"Am I willing to stand up and speak out on behalf of the powerless in our culture?"[115]

One of my favorite hymns comes from the mission fields of India. "I Have Decided to Follow Jesus" is based on the last words of a man in Garo, Assam. Famed Indian Evangelist Dr. P. P. Job relates the powerful story behind the song:

About 150 years ago, there was a great revival in Wales. As a result of this, many missionaries came to north-east India to spread the Gospel. The region known as Assam was comprised of hundreds of tribes who were primitive and aggressive head-hunters. Into these hostile and aggressive communities, came a group of missionaries from the American Baptist Missions spreading the message of love, peace and hope in Jesus Christ. Naturally, they were not welcomed. One missionary succeeded in converting a man, his wife, and two children. This man's faith proved contagious and many villagers began to accept Christianity. Angry, the village chief summoned all the villagers. He then called the family who had first converted to renounce their faith in public or face execution. Moved by the Holy Spirit, the man instantly composed a song that became famous down the years. He sang:

"I have decided to follow Jesus. I have decided to follow Jesus. I have decided to follow Jesus. No turning back, no turning back."

Enraged at the refusal of the man, the chief ordered his archers to arrow down the two children. As both boys lay twitching on the floor, the chief asked, "Will you deny your faith? You have lost both your children. You will lose your wife too."

But the man sang these words in reply:

"Though no one joins me, still I will follow. Though no one joins me, still I will follow. Though no one joins me, still I will follow. No turning back, no turning back."

The chief was beside himself with fury and ordered his wife to be arrowed down. In a moment she joined her two children in death. Now he asked for the last time, "I will give you one more opportunity to deny your faith and live." In the face of death the man sang the final memorable lines:

"The cross before me, the world behind me. The cross before me, the world behind me. The cross before me, the world behind me. No turning back, no turning back."

He was shot dead like the rest of his family. But with their deaths, a miracle took place. The chief who had ordered the killings was moved by the faith of the man. He wondered, "Why should this man, his wife and two children die for a Man who lived in a far-away land on another continent some 2,000 years ago? There must be some remarkable power behind the family's faith, and I too want to taste that faith."

In a spontaneous confession of faith, he declared, "I too belong to Jesus Christ!" When the crowd heard this from the mouth of their chief, the whole village accepted Christ as their Lord and Saviour.

The song is based on the last words of Nokseng, a man from the Garo tribe of Assam (now Meghalaya and some in Assam), India. It is today the song of the Garo people.[116]

Like Polycarp, Bonhoeffer, Martin King, Pastor Pinckney and untold others, Nokseng now wears the "Victor's Crown." Death will never again harm him!

Study Questions

Chapter 6: "When Persecution Causes You Pain"

1. According to *The Voice of the Martyrs* magazine, how many nations in the world today are violently persecuting believers?

2. Who was the bishop of Smyrna? Describe some of the details regarding his death. How long had he served Jesus the Christ?

3. How many verses in the book of Revelation are written to the church in Smyrna?

4. What type of person according to comments in this chapter, is a real threat to Satan's kingdom?

5. What famous hymn was composed by a man in India as he witnessed the persecution and death of his wife and children?

6. What miracle took place as this man, singing the final lines of the hymn, was shot to death?

7

Conclusion

Ours is a music loving family. Some of our most joyful times are when we gather around the piano as Gina plays a familiar hymn, or when we listen as Josh performs a newly composed worship song. We all join in singing. But it's difficult to sing when you're in pain. There is always the danger of losing your song in the midst of your painful struggle.

Max Lucado's well known story of "Chippie the Parakeet" helps illustrate this reality:

> Chippie, the parakeet, never saw it coming. One second he was peacefully perched in his cage, and the next, he was sucked in, washed up, and blown over. You see, the problems began when Chippie's owner decided to clean Chippie's cage with a vacuum cleaner. So she removed the attachment from the end of the hose and stuck it in the cage, and at that time the phone rang, and so she turned to pick it up. She barely said hello when, swoop, Chippie got sucked in. The bird owner gasped, put down the phone, turned off the vacuum, opened the bag; and there was Chippie still alive but stunned. And since the bird was covered with dust and soot, she grabbed him, raced him to the bathroom, turned on the faucet, held Chippie

under the running water and then realizing that Chippie was soaked and shivering. She did what any compassionate bird owner would do; she reached for the hair drier and blasted the pet with hot air, and poor Chippie never knew what hit him.

A few days after the trauma, the reporter who had initially written about this event contacted Chippie's owner to see how the bird was recovering. 'Well,' she replied, 'Chippie doesn't sing much anymore; he just sits and stares.'[117]

I want to conclude this book by helping you learn how *not* to be like Chippie. Getting 'sucked in, washed up, and blown over'—and the pain which results from these types of experiences—can easily make it difficult to maintain your song. There have been many instances when the people of God lost their song (Ps. 137:1-4).

However, God's "amazing grace" is available to His children at all times. I am a witness to this fact. Throughout this *Primer* I've tried to be very honest about the most painful episodes in my life. Though I've often been tempted to throw in the towel, walk away, and vow to never again sing of God's goodness, His grace has sustained me and to this very day, there's still a song of praise in my heart and on my lips.

The point of this book is that life is very painful at times. Christians are not immune from trials. As a matter of fact, you are either in a trial right now, you just came out of a trial, or you're headed into a trial, and there's no way around it. How we navigate these inescapable trials will largely determine what kind of people we become and what kind of legacy we will leave.

What we desperately need in such times is wisdom. But where can such wisdom be found? The New Testament contains only one letter that can be classified as "wisdom literature." It is the general letter ascribed to Jesus's own brother.[118]

It is a letter focusing on the 'nasty now and now,' a treatise on practical Christian living. It's an epistle for those in pain.

Lessons from the Brother of Jesus

Yes, Jesus had a brother—a half-brother. They had the same mother, but different fathers. His half-brother's name was James, and he wrote to a group of people who, because of painful circumstances, had almost lost their song. James knew these people well. He had been their pastor at the first church ever established, the church in Jerusalem. James was the pastor of the people of God who were undergoing a tremendous trial and persecution at the hands of a madman, a terrorist— the Osama bin Laden of his day. His name: Saul of Tarsus. Acts 8:1 says that Saul, acting like a wild animal, began to persecute the Church without regard to age or gender; locking up the people of God; persecuting the people of God; even overseeing the death of the first martyr, Stephen.

As a result of this persecution, the Bible says that the Church was scattered throughout the Greco-Roman world. As a matter of fact, the word translated *scattered* (*diaspora*) means "to pick up seed and toss it in the air."[119] It was as if a gust of wind had blown in and scattered the Church abroad. Because of this, James is concerned about his congregation. Under inspiration, he picks up a pen, puts it to parchment, and writes these words: "James, a bondservant of God and of the Lord Jesus Christ, to the twelve tribes which are scattered abroad ..." And then he begins to talk to them about *how not to lose their song* in the midst of the difficulties they're facing.

> My brothers, count it all joy when you fall into various trials, knowing that the testing of your faith produces patience. But let patience have its perfect work, that you may be perfect and complete, mature, lacking nothing. If any of you lacks wisdom, let him ask of

God, who gives to all men liberally and without reproach, and it will be given to him. But let him ask in
faith, with no doubting, for he who doubts is like a
wave of the sea driven and tossed by the wind. Let
not that man suppose that he will receive anything
from the Lord; he is a double-minded man, unstable
in all his ways.

And then in verse 12 James recalls a previously unre-
corded beatitude. It's not recorded in the Gospels, but James
recalls it: "Blessed is the man who endures trials, temptations,
difficulties; for when he has been approved, when he's passed
the test, he will receive the crown of life which the Lord has
promised to those who love Him" (translation mine).

How do you get through painful trials without losing your
song? James gives us four verbs that serve as a call to action.
They are among the fifty imperatives in the Greek language
used in this letter. James does not suggest; he commands.
These are four things we are *commanded* to do in order to
maintain our song.

Count it All Joy

He says the **first** thing we need to do when (and not 'if')
we encounter trials is to "*count* it all joy" (Jas. 1:2). The Greek
word translated as "count" is *logizomai*. It literally means "to
write something down." The word comes to us from the
world of accounting or bookkeeping. We are familiar with the
English transliteration, logistics. To paraphrase, James says,
"When you're going through a difficult time and you feel like
you're about to lose your song, sit down and take out a ledger
and write this down: 'I will rejoice!'" Count it all joy. You must
make a choice to rejoice.

Do you know that there's a difference between joy and
happiness? Happiness comes from the word *happenstance* or

happenings, and is determined by the outside in. You're happy if circumstances are going your way, if things are looking good, if everything's favorable. It's very superficial and very fleeting.

But 'joy' does not come from the outside in; it comes from the inside out. Joy chooses to sing in the midnight hour (Acts 16:25).

James paints a picture of someone walking along in life. Everything is going great, and all of the sudden you "fall into"—almost as if the bottom drops out of your life—you "fall into" (*perpipto* in Greek means to fall into a trap) *different kinds* of trials. The expression used here means variegated trials: trials of different colors.[120] Perhaps it's a trial of your finances: too much month at the end of your money. Or you might be up against some physical difficulty in your life. You might be going through a difficulty with a family member: perhaps a prodigal son or daughter. Perhaps you feel forsaken by your friends. It could even be as serious as losing your faith in God. The reality is that Christians are not immune from these painful tests of faith. As a matter of fact, the audience to whom James addresses his letter are experiencing all of these different shades of trials. As Wiersbe observes,

> As you read the epistle of James, you discover that these Jewish Christians were having some problems in their personal lives and in their church fellowship. For one thing, they were going through difficult testings. They were also facing temptations to sin. Some of the believers were catering to the rich, while others were being robbed by the rich. Church members were competing for offices in the church, particularly teaching offices. One of the major problems in the church was a failure on the part of many to live what they professed to believe. Furthermore, the tongue was a serious problem, even to the point of creating wars and divisions in the assembly. Worldliness was

another problem. Some of the members were diso-
beying God's Word and were sick physically because
of it, and some were straying away from the Lord and
the church.[121]

What do you do when you encounter trials? Do you
choose to rejoice? Many believers have chosen to complain.
Instead of being humbly grateful, they've become grumbly
hateful. I have often encountered very angry and bitter people in church services. As a matter of fact, some of the mean-
est people I've ever met attend church services every week.
The painful trials of life have embittered them. They have
long ago stopped singing. Church has become, for them, a social event: a country club with a steeple on top. They sit, soak,
and sour. Their facial expression tells all: a face so long it looks
like they could stand straight-legged and lick buttermilk out
of a gopher hole and never move an inch! They are miserable
and in turn, make everyone around them miserable. They
have failed the test. Like Chippie, they've lost their song.

I want to challenge you to make a different choice. It is a
choice based on faith and not feelings. It is an act of a Spirit-
filled will. It is a choice to praise God in the midst of every
situation, not *for* every situation. Not every situation comes
from God! Some painful trials come straight out of the pit of
hell. But even when the source of our trial is the enemy, we
have to learn to stand and withstand *joyfully*. So, we don't give
God thanks *for* everything. We give God thanks *in the midst*
of everything. We don't praise God because our lives are going well; we praise God because He's God! So, it matters not
what is raging about us; He deserves our praise! Thus, the first
thing you have to determine is this: I will rejoice. Count it all
joy when painful trials come against you. Remember that
these difficulties come to test you. God uses these difficulties
to bring the *best* out of you. The enemy uses them to bring the

worst out of you. One of my British friends put it this way: Christians are like tea bags. You never know what flavor they have until you put them in hot water! How true this is! Make a choice to rejoice and again I say, "Rejoice!"

Know that the Trial of Your Faith Produces Patience

Now notice the **second** verb in verse 3. It's the word, *knowing.* Christians know something that lost people don't know. Where do we know it? We know it in our *knower!* We know it in our spirit. The word translated "know," *ginosko* means to know something by personal experience.[122] We know that God can be trusted because we've experienced His faithfulness. We know it in the innermost part of our being which has come alive by the Spirit of God. Because we have been born again, the Spirit has given us an assurance, a sense of confidence which confounds a lost and confused world.

When your friends at the office see that in spite of the fact that you're going through severe trials you exude a joy and confidence which they don't possess, it opens up a tremendous door of opportunity to "sing" the song of salvation through Christ. Many people in our world lack the inner fortitude to be able to handle the difficulties of life. They often turn to drugs or alcohol or extramarital affairs. Sometimes they disappear into a virtual world of erotic fantasy. They desperately need to see and hear a living testimony to the faithfulness of God in the midst of the chaotic world in which we live. Don't let the devil steal your song!

The assurance we possess is not escapism. It is the confidence that comes through knowing that what we are going through is producing something in us, namely, *endurance.* The word *hupomone* literally means, the ability to bear up under any circumstance. It describes what we might call 'staying power.' The word was used in antiquity to describe an evergreen: a tree which could grow in any and every climate. It is an active and not a passive posture in the midst of painful suffering. In Classical Greek, the word was used for a person "leaning into the wind." So, this patience produced by way of trials is not the 'grin and bear it' type of attitude. Rather, it is the confident expectation that what we are enduring will actually benefit us and those around us. The trial comes to make us stronger and more like our Lord. It is a test.

In addition to serving as an evangelist, I am also a college professor. This means I often give my students tests. I intend for them to take the test by themselves. I do not speak to them when I administer a test. I am not giving them the test in order to embarrass them. I intend to measure just how much they have paid attention to my instructions and teaching and the reading assignments I have given them to do. My ultimate goal is for them to come through the test with greater confidence in what they know about the subject they are studying. Likewise, in the Christian life, *a faith which cannot be tested is a faith which cannot be trusted!*

This does not mean I enjoy the trial. I may not like what I'm going through. I don't find what I'm going through to be fun. It's a difficult thing, and I wish it were not so; nevertheless, it is. And so, I must confidently make this choice: I'm going to rejoice in the Lord, knowing that God is going to take this terrible thing and use it in my life to make me more like Jesus. By His grace, I can endure every trial that comes into my life! Whatever comes, I'm not going to lose my song. You see, if the devil can steal your song, then you won't sing the song of salvation that the world so desperately needs to hear.

Let Patience Have Its Perfect Work

The **third** key action word is the word *let* or *allow*. "*Let* patience have its perfect work so that you may be perfect and mature and complete, lacking nothing" (Jas. 1:4). As counterintuitive as it may sound, God *requires* your cooperation in His plan for your life! In order to benefit from life's various trials, you must allow the process to run its full course. Matthew Henry encourages us in this matter:

> Let us give it leave to work, and it will work wonders in a time of trouble. We must let it have its perfect work. When we hear all that God appoints, and as long as he appoints, and we not only bear troubles, but rejoice in them, then patience hath its perfect work. When the work of patience is complete, then the Christian is entire, and nothing will be wanting.[123]

So do not run from God! Do not fight with God! Those who try to box with God will always lose; their arms are just too short. We must learn to let God do what He wants to do in our lives, namely, to produce in us the kind of endurance of faith which is able to bear up under any circumstance in life and still be fruitful for the kingdom of God. You don't have to lose your song!

Ask of God

And then, last, James says that we must *ask*. "If any of you lacks wisdom let him ask of God" (Jas. 1:5). We ask God for wisdom. In the Bible, wisdom is the ability to see the trial from God's vantage point and to know how to respond properly. "Philosophy may instruct men to remain calm under their troubles; but Christianity teaches them to be joyful."[124] Much of this book has been a search for God's wisdom in determining the source of painful trials. Perhaps the pain you are suffering is the result of someone hurting you deeply. If so, forgive them. Don't rehearse the pain or nurse the pain. Let God reverse the pain and use the pain to make you more loving, tender and compassion toward fellow sufferers. Is the pain the result of an attack of the enemy? If so, learn to withstand his assault. Has God revealed to you that you are suffering the consequences of your own sinful or foolish choices? Perhaps repentance is called for in this circumstance. Or are you suffering a kind of pain common to all people everywhere throughout all of human history: a pain that has come into the world as a result of the Fall. In this case, know that this *Now Season* will soon give way to the *New Season* of the resurrection and full manifestation of the children of God!

When we ask God for insight into the source of and proper response to our trials, we must do so in faith. We must trust the heart of our Father. When we can't trace His hand, we must trust His heart. We must believe the promise of Romans 8:28. We must not be the, "Mr. Looking Both Ways" of Bunyan's *Pilgrim's Progress.* James calls such a person, "two-souled" or "double-minded." And it is comforting to know that Father will never scold or reprimand one of His wisdom-seeking children.

Keep on Singing

In the aftermath of the Metro Church bus crash, thousands of people spontaneously began showing up on the church campus. We never called a special meeting. They crowded our auditorium, standing all the way around the exterior of the building. Do you know what they began to do? They didn't come to philosophize about the problem of evil. They didn't come angrily seeking someone to blame for the crash. They chose instead to sing. They stood for hours, tears running down their cheeks, hands lifted toward Heaven, hearts heavy with pain—and they sang.

Michael Freeman's father, Scott, sang. When I saw him on the platform, microphone in hand, tears dripping off his cheeks onto the floor, I asked, "Scott, are you sure you can do this?" He said, "Pastor, I do it every Sunday. I'm going to do it in the good times and in the bad." His fourteen-year-old son was killed in the bus crash. Scott took a microphone and stood on the stage, lifted his hands toward heaven, and *sang*! And day after day, thousands of people came to sing. Over three hundred people came to Christ in three days; we baptized almost all of them. A mighty revival had broken out in the midst of the pain we were going through!

When you don't know what to do, *sing*! When your heart is broken, *sing*! When you're going through trials, *sing* the praises of your God! We serve a God who can take the most difficult of days and turn them into something good. That's our God!

Jesus was a singer. Have you ever thought about that? Jesus sang. The Bible says on the night He was betrayed, when it was just Him and His closest followers, that they had supper. He took some bread, and (allow me to paraphrase) He said, "Boys, this is what they're going to do to me." And He took the bread and began to break it, and He said, "Boys, they're going to take a 'cat of nine tails,' and they're going to shred my skin until it falls from my backside like red ribbons and my bones are exposed." Jesus grew up in a culture that was very familiar with crucifixion. He knew what it was to be crucified, and He knew it was coming. He predicted it throughout His ministry. He said, "They're going to beat me until I don't look human. They're going to spit in my face and rip my beard out by the roots." How did He know that? Because it's prophesied in the Old Testament. "They're going to pierce my hands and feet. All my bones are going to come out of joint and stare up at me." I'm sure they wept as Jesus took a cup, and said, "Boys, this cup is my blood. They're going to put a crown of thorns on my head and beat Me in the head with a stick until the capillaries burst and my blood is spilled all over the ground, all over my body. I'm going to look like a complete and total mess. I'll look like a piece of hamburger meat, and every time you eat this bread and drink this cup, I want you to remember that I love you and that I'm laying my life down for you." Jesus knew what was coming. The Bible says that after they ate the bread and drank the cup that they stood up and *sang*. I am most certain that Jesus himself was in charge of the song service that night! He led them in a hymn and afterward they went out into the dark night.

Jesus, when facing the most difficult trial, which He likened unto drinking a cup (of which he would later say, "Oh, God, if there's any way that I can bypass it, if there's any other way, Lord, I don't want to drink the cup of suffering, shame, sin and separation; but nevertheless, God, not my will but Your will be done)," chose to sing! Jesus never lost his song.

When California State officials said that Christians gathered for worship during the pandemic could not sing, I knew they were vastly underestimating the power of our faith![125] Christians *always sing!* We sing from the heights of mountain-top experiences. We sing when passing "through the valley of the shadow of death" (Ps. 23:4). We know that just as a shadow of a dog cannot bite you, the shadow of a car cannot run you over nor can the shadow of a bullet kill you, that "the valley of the shadow of death" itself cannot stop you or cause you to lose your song.

Let me end this book the same way I started it. Following Jesus does not mean that life will always be easy for you. Christianity is not an escape from pain. In fact, in many ways, it is just the opposite. It is an invitation to enter into the painful "fellowship of His [Christ's] sufferings" (Phil. 3:9). Christians believe that God is so powerful that He has the ability to take us through the very valley of the shadow of death and bring us out on the other side: better, not bitter; victorious, not victims.

This is our understanding of pain.

ABOUT THE AUTHOR

Dr. Scott Camp has a unique blend of life experiences that give him a powerful, relevant ministry to reach the unreachable with the message of Christ. He was the product of a teenage pregnancy, alcoholism, and a broken home. His own drug and alcohol abuse led to a felony charge, and he was arrested while in high school. It was there that Scott committed his life to following Christ and shortly thereafter was called to preach. Dr. Camp has served in a variety of capacities since entering vocational ministry in 1982, including student pastor, evangelist, church planter, college professor, and Dean of Students. He has been the Sr. Pastor of four growing congregations, which include First Baptist Church of Sachse, TX; Metro Church of Garland, TX; First Baptist Church of Mansfield, TX; and most recently, Fellowship of Joy in Grand Prairie, TX.

Dr. Camp now travels extensively throughout the United States, Eastern Europe, Mexico, South America, Pakistan and the continent of Africa preaching at churches, city-wide crusades, and conferences. He has been featured as a program guest with the Billy Graham Crusade. Dr. Camp currently serves as the Faculty Chair of Evangelism at SUM Bible College and Theological Seminary in Oakland, CA

Thousands have responded to the gospel under his ministry worldwide. He has ministered to international audiences in person as well as via television and radio broadcasts. His ministry has been covered in various newspaper magazine articles including the *Dallas Morning News* and *Ft. Worth Star Telegram*. He has also preached at numerous state evangelism/youth evangelism and pastor's conferences across the nation for various denominational and interdenominational groups.

Dr. Camp holds a Master of Arts in Theology from Criswell College, graduating Summa Cum Laude. In addition, he holds a Master of Divinity from Southwestern Assemblies of God University and a Master of Theology degree from Southwestern Baptist Theological Seminary. In 2007, he was awarded an honorary Doctor of Divinity degree from St. Thomas Christian College in Jacksonville, Florida. In addition, Scott has done doctoral studies at Southwestern Baptist Theological Seminary, The Assemblies of God Theological Seminary, Baylor University, and Southern Evangelical Seminary.

Scott married his wife, Gina, in 1988, and they have four children: Sarah, Dillon, Joshua, and Madison. Gina has taught music, directed children's choirs, and has also been a featured vocalist and worship leader at various conferences.

www.ScottCamp.org

DISCOVER JOY
Scott Camp Ministries

LEAVE A WELL

Someone said, "When you go through the valley, leave a well." In other words, when Christians go through difficult times and experience God's help and strength, we ought to leave a source of blessing for those travelers who will come behind us.

If this volume has been a blessing to you, please consider taking a few moments to leave a "Review" at site where you purchased this book. Leaving a review of at least 25 words will help others find this book and its message of hope for them.

You can follow this link to leave a review for *A Primer On Pain* at Amazon.

St. Catherine's Well, Glenwood Mission Inn,
Riverside, CA., Courtesy NYPL, Circa 1918

FRANKLIN PUBLISHING

The goal of Franklin Publishing is to enable Pastors, Evangelists, Missionaries, and Christian leaders and presenters to become published authors. Becoming a published author expands your influence and builds your ministry. You can write the book or sermon series which God has laid on your heart. We can walk that road with you. Start by downloading our free writers publishing guide.

www.FranklinPublishing.org

Come and visit our Facebook page and be sure to like and follow us to keep up with writing tips and new developments.

www.facebook.com/FranklinPublishing

Notes

Preface:

1 C. S. Lewis, *A Grief Observed* in C. S. Lewis Signature Classics (New York: Harper Collins, 2017, orig. pub. 1961), 668.

Introduction:

2 This differentiates my *Primer* from Phillip Yancey's helpful volume, *Where's God When it Hurts?* (Grand Rapids, MI: Zondervan, 1990). Yancey deals primarily with the nature of physical pain.

3 For an excellent overview of the various answers Christian philosophers have offered for the "Problem of Evil," see Kenneth D. Boa and Robert M. Bowman, Jr., *Faith Has Its Reasons* (Colorado Springs: NavPress, 2001), 120-123; 212-213; 331-334; 427-429; 528-529.

4 This differentiates my *Primer* from C.S. Lewis's classic text, *The Problem of Pain* (San Francisco: HarperOne, 2015), which is far more philosophical in nature.

Chapter 1:

5 Gary Smalley, *The Blessing* (New York: Pocket Books, 1986), 27.

6 C. S. Lewis, *The Problem of Pain* (1940; repr., San Francisco: HarperSanFrancisco, 2001), 91.

7 All Scripture citations, unless otherwise noted, are from the New King James Version.

8 Charles R. Swindoll, *Joseph: A Man of Integrity and Forgiveness* (Dallas: Insight for Living, 1998), 5.

9 John Calvin, in *A Treasury of Evangelical Writings*, compiled and edited by David Otis Fuller (Grand Rapids, MI: Kregel, 1974), 198.

10 See Gregory A. Boyd, *Satan and the Problem of Evil: Constructing a Trinitarian Warfare Theodicy* (Downers Grove, IL: IVP, 2001). Boyd reminds us of this when he writes, "To be sure, God can use evil agents to fulfill his purposes, and He always works to bring good out of evil. But God's specific way of responding to a particular evil must not be confused with God specifically ordaining or allowing a particular evil" (205).

11 Swindoll, *Joseph*, 25.

12 William Wilson, *Wilson's Old Testament Word Studies* (McLean, VA: MacDonald Publishing, 1975), 174.

---

[13] "Forgive," in *New International Dictionary of New Testament Theology*, edited by Colin Brown (Grand Rapids, MI: Zondervan, 1980), 697.

[14] Henry Blackaby and Claude V. King, *Experiencing God: Knowing and Doing the Will of God* (Nashville: LifeWay Press, 1990). Blackaby notes that "Anytime God leads you to do something that has God-sized dimensions, you will face a crisis of belief. When you face a crisis of belief, what you do next reveals what you really believe about God" (108). This was so in Joseph's case. He was confronted with a crisis of belief that involved a choice to either forgive or continue to live in bitterness. In this case, the viability of the people of God was at stake. Imagine if Joseph had killed his brothers. There would be no people of God called "Israel."

[15] Without question, Christ's suffering was unique. Various theories associated with the Atonement are linked to His suffering, such as penal substitutionary atonement, ransom theory, governmental theory, *Christus Victor*, liberation theory, cruciform forgiveness, and the moral example theory. For detailed treatments of various models of the Atonement, see Peter Schmiechen, *Saving Power: Theories of Atonement and Forms of the Church* (Grand Rapids, MI: Eerdmans, 2005); Fisher Humphries, *The Death of Christ* (Nashville: Broadman, 1978); and John R. W. Stott, *The Cross of Christ* (Downers Grove, IL: IVP, 2006).

Our suffering is not of the same quality and is in no way the basis upon which God chooses to forgive sinners. And yet, there is a sense in which we share in the fellowship of Christ's suffering (Phil. 3:10) and in which we are called to follow in His steps (1 Pet. 2:21).

[16] For a more detailed account of my experience with the Holy Spirit, see my book, *A Primer on Power: Discovering the Dynamic Ministry of the Holy Spirit* (Greenville, TX: Franklin Publishing, 2016).

[17] For an excellent treatment on breaking free from generational strongholds, see Neil T. Anderson, *The Bondage Breaker: Overcoming Negative Thoughts, Irrational Feelings, and Habitual Sins* (Eugene, OR: Harvest House Publishing, 2000).

[18] Historically, the Christian Church has taught that the Lord Jesus Christ is one person who simultaneously possesses two natures: true humanity and true divinity. This doctrine is called the hypostatic union. [19] The similarities between Joseph and Christ have been noted by several Church Fathers. This method of reading the Bible is called prosopological exegesis. It is a highly spiritual and Christocentric method of biblical interpretation. For a collection of the early Fathers' prosopological commentaries on Scripture (and for comparisons between Joseph and Christ especially), see *The Ancient Christian Commentary on Scripture: Old Testament Vol. 2, Genesis 12-50*, edited by Mark Sheridan (Downers Grove: IVP, 2002).

Cyril of Alexander makes an explicit connection by asserting that Joseph receiving his family back again was a prophetic glimpse into an eschatological event wherein Jesus will again receive Israel (and all people willing to come):

> This narrative is a clear sign that the Israelites
> themselves, by coming back in the latter times of
> the world, will be received by Christ, that is,
> when they will be in accord with the new people,
> that is symbolized, as I have said, by Benjamin.
> In addition, the inheritance we hope for will be
> given to us only by the holy fathers. As those
> who died in the faith, as the wise Paul says, 'did
> not receive what was promised since God had
> provided something better so they would not,
> apart from us, be made perfect' (307).

[20] See Corrie ten Boom, John Sherrill, and Elizabeth Sherrill, *The Hiding Place: The Triumphant True Story of Corrie ten Boom* (Old Tappan, NJ: Chosen Books, 1971). Corrie ten Boom recalls the moving story of her sister Betsie's death at the hands of a Nazi prison guard. Years later, the guard came to Christ at a meeting where Corrie told Betsie's story.

Chapter 2:

[21] "Church Bus Crash Kills Five," *The Dallas Morning News*, June 25, 2002, https://www2.ljworld.com/news/2002/jun/25/church_bus_crash/.

Chapter 3:

[22] See John Calvin's *The Institutes of the Christian Religion*, Christian Classics Ethereal Library, 1536, trans. by Henry Beveridge, 1845, accessed July 4, 2020, https://www.ccel.org/ccel/calvin/institutes.html.

[23] "The Westminster Confession of Faith (1647)," Ligonier Ministries, accessed July 4, 2020, https://www.ligonier.org/learn/articles/westminster-confession-faith/. This document codified Calvinistic doctrine, and it describes God's sovereignty as "power over His creatures," which includes His power to "freely, and unchangeably ordain whatsoever comes to pass" (WCF 3.1-7).

[24] See Gordon H. Clark, "God and Evil," in *Religion, Reason and Revelation* (Jefferson, MD: The Trinity Foundation 1986).

[25] Michael Green, *I Believe in Satan's Downfall* (Grand Rapids, MI: Eerdmans, 1981), 20.

[26] Theologian Karl Barth has described the devil, demons, and evil as "nothing,'" by which he means that they exist as the uncreated "no" to God's created "yes." They are the anti-creation, the shadow-dwellers, who exist absent from the light of God's creation. Barth asserts, "God has not created them, and therefore, they are not creaturely. They exist only as God affirms Himself and the creature and thus pronounces a necessary 'no'." See Karl Barth, *Church Dogmatics* (Edinburgh: T&T Clark, 1960), 3.3.523.

[27] W. A. Criswell, *The Great Doctrines of the Bible*, Vol. 7 (Grand Rapids, MI: Zondervan, 1987), 88.

[28] Boyd, *Satan and the Problem of Evil*, 314.

[29] See Bob Larson, *The Day the Music Died* (Carol Stream: Creation House, 1972).

[30] William Langley, "A Focused Biblical Study of Spiritual Warfare and Its Implications for the Local Church," PhD diss (Shreveport: Louisiana Baptist University, 2010).

[31] For issues involving the date, genre, purpose, and various interpretations of Job, see chapter 14 on Job in Richard S. Hess, *The Old Testament: A Historical, Theological, and Critical Introduction* (Grand Rapids, MI: Baker, 2016), 393-416.

[32] "Theodicy," in *Baker's Dictionary of Theology*, ed. Everett F. Harrison (Grand Rapids, MI: Baker, 1960), 517.

[33] See my friend Walter Hallam's book by the same title, *The Big Why: Understanding Adversity and Transforming Your Troubles into Triumphs* (Tulsa: Harrison House, 2010).

[34] C. S. Lewis, *The Screwtape Letters*, vol. 6 of *The C. S. Lewis Signature Classics (8-Volume Box Set): An Anthology.* San Francisco and New York: HarperOne, 2017.

[35] See Carl Raschke, *The Next Reformation: Why Evangelicals Must Embrace Postmodernity* (Grand Rapids, MI: Baker, 2004).

[36] See Jürgen Moltmann, *The Crucified God: The Cross of Christ as the Foundation and Criticism of Christian Theology* (Minneapolis: Fortress Press, 1993).

[37] Jody Deen, *Finding God in the Evening News: A Broadcast Journalist Looks Beyond the Headlines* (Grand Rapids, MI: Revell, 2004), 26.

38 Warren Wiersbe, *The Wiersbe Bible Commentary: Old Testament* (Colorado Springs: David C. Cook, 2007), 827.

39 Ibid., 828.

40 Ibid.

41 This idea runs contrary to the thought of Classical Theists like Thomas Aquinas and their doctrine of "impassibility." Impassibility is "the doctrine that God is not capable of being acted upon or affected emotionally by anything in creation." See "Impassibility," in *Evangelical Dictionary of Theology*, edited by Walter A. Elwell (Grand Rapids: Baker, 1984), 553.

42 Paul Tournier, *Reflections* (New York: Harper & Row, 1976), 142.

43 In other words, the "hidden God" became the "revealed God." The *Oxford Handbook of Martin Luther's Theology* helpfully explains this: "Luther's distinction of the hidden and revealed God (*Deus absconditus, Deus revelatus*) permeates his theology. God revealed is ultimately the justifying God who recreates sinners through his word of forgiveness." See *Oxford Handbook of Martin Luther's Theology*, ed. Robert Kolb, Irene Dingel, and L'ubomír Batka (Oxford: 2014), 10.1093 oxfordhb/9780199604708.013.034.

In other words, Christ was made to know suffering on the Cross. The Cross is both a word of comfort and the means of salvation for sufferers and sinners like you and me.

44 *The Matthew Henry Commentary* (Grand Rapids, MI: Zondervan, 1961), 543-544.

45 Ibid., 530.

46 Mark Sheridan and Marco Conti, eds., *Job*, vol. VI of The *Ancient Christian Commentary on Scripture: Old Testament*, gen. ed. Thomas C. Oden (Downers Grove: IVP, 2002).

47 See Boyd, *Satan and the Problem of Evil*, 225.

48 Holly Meehan, public post to Facebook, (June 23, 2012, 10:51 AM), https://www.facebook.com/photo.php?fbid=3699467039326&set=a.1041002579376&type=3&theater.

Chapter 4:

[49] Dietrich Bonhoeffer, *Temptation* (New York: MacMillan, 1953), 116-17.

[50] Matthew Henry, *The Matthew Henry Commentary*, 341.

[51] Taken from Chuck Swindoll, "Autopsy of a Moral Fall," chapel sermon delivered at Dallas Theological Seminary, December 14, 2016. Quotation begins at 43:16, https://youtu.be/WzqG-98uRU0.

[52] The Christian Library, *The Confessions of St. Augustine* (Uhrichsville: Barbour, 1984), 26.

[53] Cornelius Plantinga, *Not the Way It's Supposed to Be: A Breviary of Sin* (Grand Rapids, MI: Eerdmans, 1995), 46.

[54] Ibid., 53.

[55] For a full discussion on the meaning of the word *hesed*, see Ralph L. Smith, *Old Testament Theology: History, Method, and Message* (Nashville: Broadman & Holman, 1993), 196-7. Smith explains, "*Hesed* contains two basic elements: one is the idea of strength, loyalty, and steadfastness. The other is the idea of kindness, pity, mercy, and grace. Perhaps 'devotion' (Jer. 2:2) captures both elements in the word" (197).

[56] Alexander Whyte, *Bible Characters* (Grand Rapids, MI: Zondervan, 1952), 245.

[57] Phillip Keller, "Chapter 8: Thy Rod and Thy Staff They Comfort Me," in *A Shepherd Looks at the 23rd Psalm* (Grand Rapids, MI: Zondervan, 1970).

[58] Roy Hession, *The Calvary Road* (Fort Washington, PA: CLC Publications, 1950), 21-3.

[59] John Calvin, *Commentary on the Book of Psalms*, trans. James Anderson (Grand Rapids, MI: Baker 1998), 5:2:306.

[60] Karl Menninger, *Whatever Became of Sin?* (New York: Hawthorn Books, 1973).

[61] *Wilson's Old Testament Word Studies*, 458.

[62] C. F. Keil and F. Delitzsch, *Commentary on the Old Testament*, trans. James Martin (Grand Rapids, MI: Eerdmans, 1982), 2:383.

[63] Henry, *The Matthew Henry Commentary*, 630.

[64] Mitchell Dahood, *The Anchor Bible Commentary: Psalms II, 51-100*, ed. William Foxwell Albright and David Noel Freedman (Garden City, NY: Double Day, 1968), 17:3.

[65] Erasmus, "Concerning the Immense Mercy of God," in *The Essential Erasmus*, trans. John P. Dolan (New York: Meridian, 1983), 253.

[66] D. T. Niles, *That They May Have Life* (New York: Harper & Brothers, 1951), 96.

[67] Calvin, *Commentary on the Psalms*, 302.

[68] Makoto Fujimura, "Kintsugi Generation," May 5, 2019, accessed July 18, 2020, https://www.makotofujimura.com/writings/kintsugi-generation/.

Chapter 5:

[69] See Elisabeth Kübler-Ross, *On Death and Dying: What the Dying Have to Teach Doctors, Nurses, Clergy and their own* Families (New York: Macmillan, 19690).

[70] John R. Stott, *The Cross of Christ* (Downers Grove, IL: InterVarsity Press, 1986), 311.

[71] Warren Wiersbe, *The Warren Wiersbe Bible Commentary: New Testament* (Colorado Springs: David C. Cook, 2007), 429-32.

[72] Robert Browning Hamilton, "Along the Road," Poetry Nook, accessed August 7, 2020, https://www.poetrynook.com/poem/along-road.

[73] A. T. Roberston, *Word Pictures in the New Testament, Vol. IV* (Nashville: Broadman Press, 1931), 376.

[74] Ibid., 375.

[75] Dale Moody, *Acts-1 Corinthians*, vol. 10 of *The Broadman Bible Commentary* (Nashville: Broadman Press, 1970), 218.

[76] N. T. Wright, *Paul for Everyone: Romans, Part 1*, Chap. 1-8 (Louisville: Westminster John Knox Press, 2004), 151-2.

[77] Francis Schaeffer, "A Christian View of Philosophy and Culture," in *The Complete Works of Francis Schaeffer: A Christian Worldview*, vol. 1 (Wheaton: Crossway, 1982), 102.

[78] This is beautifully allegorized in John Bunyan's classic, *The Pilgrim's Progress*.

[79] Everett Harrison, "Romans," in *Zondervan NIV Bible Commentary*, vol. 2: New Testament, ed. Kenneth L. Barker and John R. Kohlenberger III (Grand Rapids, MI: Zondervan, 1994), 564.

[80] Dale Moody, *Broadman Bible Commentary*, 219.

[81] A. T. Robertson, *Word Pictures in the New Testament, vol. VI: The General Epistles and the Revelation of John* (Nashville: Broadman Press, 1933), 376.

[82] Might Jesus have experienced this Spirit-inspired groan? The Bible records that when He stood at the gravesite of his best friend, Lazarus, He groaned in His spirit (John 11:33). Perhaps, in this deeply painful experience, as He lost control of His emotions and joined Mary and Martha in a mournful wail (v. 35), the Spirit took

over and began communicating to the Father the pathos of the Son. Did the Spirit then communicate the will of the Father back to the Son regarding the revivification of Lazarus's dead body? After all, did Jesus not say earlier, "I say to you, the Son can do nothing of himself, but only what He sees the Father do; for whatever He does, the Son also does in like manner. For the Father loves the Son and shows Him all things that He himself does; and He will show Him greater works than these, that you may marvel. For as the Father raises the dead and gives life to them, even so the Son gives life to whom He will" (5:19-22). Jesus later indicates that those who believe in Him would "speak with new tongues" (Mark 16:17). This prophecy is in the context of facing difficulties in carrying out His Great Commission.

[83] Gordon D. Fee, *God's Empowering Presence: The Holy Spirit in the Letters of Paul* (Grand Rapids, MI: Baker Academic, 1994), 580-1.

[84] See my book, *A Primer on Power*, 143.

[85] Jack Hayford, *The Beauty of Spiritual Language: Unveiling the Mystery of Speaking in Tongues* (Nashville: Thomas Nelson, 1996), 138.

[86] Charles Spurgeon, *12 Sermons on the Passion and Death of Christ* (Grand Rapids, MI: Baker, 1971), 101-2.

[87] Stott, *The Cross of Christ*, 329.

Chapter 6:

[88] *The Voice of the Martyrs*, Spring Edition (Bartlesville: VOM, 2020).

[89] David E. Aune, *Word Biblical Commentary,* vol. 52, *Revelation 1-5*, ed. Ralph P. Martin (Dallas: Word Books, 1997), 161.

[90] William Barclay, *The Daily Study Bible Series, Revised Edition,* vol. 1, *The Revelation of John* (Philadelphia: Westminster Press, 1976).

[91] Eusebius, "The Death of Polycarp," in *Ecclesiastical History*, trans. C.F. Cruse (Peabody, MA: Hendrickson Publishers, 1998), 122-128.

[92] See, for example, J. Vernon McGee, *The Prophecy: Revelation Chapters 1-5*, vol. 58 of *Thru the Bible Commentary Series* (Nashville: Thomas Nelson, 1991), 76. McGee and others link these periods with the "ten days" of persecution spoken of by Jesus.

[93] W. A. Criswell, *Expository Sermons on Revelation: Five Volumes Complete and Unabridged in One* (Dallas: Criswell Publishing, 1995), 102.

[94] Barclay, *The Daily Study Bible: Revelation*, 78.

[95] Aune, *Revelation 1-5*, 161. Aune suggests several reasons for the poverty of the Smyrna Christians only to settle on the unwillingness of the church to compromise with the worship of the pagans.

[96] Ibid., 163.

[97] Eusebius, "Death of Polycarp," 122-128.

[98] John Foxe, *Foxe's Book of Martyrs*, ed. William Byron Forbush (Grand Rapids, MI: Zondervan, 1926), 9.

[99] I am fully aware that many interpreters understand the *'Aggeloi'* to whom the seven letters are addressed to be spiritual beings who observe, oversee, and perhaps guard the churches, both past and present. For a full discussion of this and other positions, see Aune, *Revelation 1-5*, 108-112.

[100] A. T. Roberston, *Word Pictures in the New Testament*, vol. VI, *The General Epistles and The Revelation of John* (Nashville: Broadman Press, 1933), 301.

[101] J. Massyngberde Ford, *The Anchor Bible*, vol. 38, *Revelation* (New York: Doubleday & Co., 1975), 394-5.

[102] Aune, *Revelation 1-5*, 163.

[103] Tertullian, *Apologeticus* L.13.

[104] Harvey Blaney, *Wesleyan Bible Commentary*, vol. VI, *Hebrews-Revelation*, ed. Charles W. Carter (Grand Rapids: Baker, 1966), 431.

[105] Dietrich Bonhoeffer, *The Cost of Discipleship*, Shepherd's Notes Christian Classics (Nashville: Broadman & Holman, 1995), 99.

[106] Barclay, *Daily Study Bible: Revelation*, 83.

[107] McGee, *Revelation 1-5*, 77.

[108] See Anne Applebaum, *Twilight of Democracy: The Seductive Lure of Authoritarianism* (Toronto: McClelland and Stewart, 2020).

[109] See Paul Alexander, *Peace to War: Shifting Alliances in the Assemblies of God*, vol. 9 of *C. Henry Smith Series*, ed. J. Denny Weaver (Telford: Cascadia Publishing, 2007).

[110] C. W. Conn, "Persecution," in *The New International Dictionary of Pentecostal and Charismatic Movements*, ed. Stanley Burgess (Grand Rapids: Zondervan, 2002), 984.

[111] Aldon D. Morris, *The Origins of the Civil Rights Movement: Black Communities Organizing for Change* (NYC: Free Press, 1984), 4-12.

[112] Helen Davidson, "Oregon College Shooting: 'He Asked Are You Christian? Then He Shot and Killed Them,'" *The Guardian*, October 2, 2015, https://www.theguardian.com/us-news/2015/oct/02/oregon-college-shooting-he- asked-are-you-christian-then-he-shot-and-killed-them.

Horowitz, Nick Corasaniti and Ashley Southall, "Nine Killed in ͜ting at Black Church in Charleston," *The New York Times,* June 17, 2015, ͜ttps://www.nytimes.com/2015/06/18/us/church-attacked-in-charleston-south-carolina.html.

[114] "Los Angeles County Church Appears Ready to Defy Court Order and Hold Indoor Services," *The Los Angeles Times,* August 16, 2020, https://www.latimes.com/california/story/2020-08-16/los-angeles-county-church-set- to-defy-court-order-hold-indoor-services.
[115] Wolfgang Gerlach, *And the Witnesses Were Silent: The Confessing Church and the Jews* (Lincoln, NE: University of Nebraska Press, 2000).

I am reminded here of the great Martin Niemoller's widely quoted poem:

"First they came for the socialists, and I did not speak out—

Because I was not a socialist.

Then they came for the trade unionists, and I did not speak out—

Because I was not a trade unionist.

Then they came for the Jews, and I did not speak out—

Because I was not a Jew.

Then they came for me—and there was no one left to speak for me" (47).

God is raising up the next Smyrna church. It may well be this generation. Are we prepared to suffer?

[116] P. P. Job, *Why God, Why?* (Faridabad: Sabina Press, 1999).

Conclusion

[117] Max Lucado, *In the Eye of the Storm: Jesus Knows How You Feel* (Nashville: Thomas Nelson, 1991), xi-xii.

[118] For various views on the authorship of the epistle, see Robert H. Gundry, *A Survey of the New Testament*, 3rd ed. (Grand Rapids, MI: Zondervan, 1994), 432.

[119] Robertson, *Word Pictures in the New Testament*, 10.

[120] Ibid., 11.

[121] Warren Wiersbe, *The Wiersbe Bible Commentary: The Complete New Testament in One Volume* (Colorado Springs: David C. Cook, 2007), 849.

[122] Robertson, *Word Pictures in the New Testament*, 12.

[123] *The Matthew Henry Commentary* (Grand Rapids, MO: Zondervan, 1961), 1930.

[124] Ibid.

[125] Dale Kasler, "Houses of worship told to 'discontinue singing' under order from Newsom as pandemic worsens," *The Sacramento Bee*, July 2, 2020, https://www. sacbee.com/news/coronavirus/article243973397.html.

Made in the USA
Monee, IL
24 September 2021